7/7 AND 21/7
DELVING INTO ROOM 101

7/7 AND 21/7
DELVING INTO ROOM 101

CLIFF TODD

Matador
9 Priory Business Park,
Wistow Road, Kibworth Beauchamp,
Leicestershire. LE8 0RX
Tel: 0116 279 2299
Email: books@troubador.co.uk
Web: www.troubador.co.uk/matador
Twitter: @matadorbooks

ISBN 978 1788039 727

British Library Cataloguing in Publication Data.
A catalogue record for this book is available from the British Library.

Printed and bound by CPI Group (UK) Ltd, Croydon, CR0 4YY
Typeset in 11pt Minion Pro by Troubador Publishing Ltd, Leicester, UK

Matador is an imprint of Troubador Publishing Ltd

To the memory of Vanessa my wife, for all that she was to me. And to Jim & Gillian, without whose encouragement I would never have seen this through.

CONTENTS

INTRODUCTION

Room 101 – in George Orwell's *Nineteen Eighty-Four*, a dread place where one's worst fears are kept, as instruments of torture and control. Popularised by the TV programme as somewhere to drop things into, anything you don't like or don't want to face. And if you don't go back in there, you won't have to face them – maybe. The thing is, for me anyway, that stuff has not actually gone away, it just sort of – lurks. Which can have its own effects, if perhaps more subtle than trying to deal head-on with whatever you're not facing.

When I retired, I was asked if I was going to write my memoirs, to which I replied, quite emphatically, no. I was done with work. My wife, Vanessa, had cancer, but it was under control, we and her doctors all thought she would have a few years in which we could do lots of stuff that we had always wanted to, and basically have some quality time together. Life had other ideas, and a few years turned into six months, when she died very suddenly. This hit me really quite hard, and my main way of coping was to do what I think I've always tended to do – tell myself to suck it up, there's nothing I can do about it, move on. But I also started writing a bit, just purely personal stuff, not for anyone to read, and it seemed to help a bit. Anyway, after a couple of years, I was more or less done with that, but I still quite liked writing, so was casting about for something a bit more specific to write about. And then I just suddenly thought about 7/7 and 21/7 – that was a very intense part of my life, which I had never really talked about much, just bits and pieces with close family and friends. Maybe I could write something about that, might even show it to some family or friends, if they were interested – there was certainly a story there. And while in the past I had written much on the subject, it was in a professional capacity, so all very objective and addressing specific questions for specific audiences. This time I could write something personal, and with no constraints, since it would be for my own benefit.

And so I started writing it. But in doing so, I was having to try and remember things that had long since been put out of my mind – and I gradually realised that actually, I had never really thought about any of it in any sort of reflective way – I had just moved through it, never looking back. So when I began, thoughts I had about personal aspects of this story started out as one thing, but as I reflected, while trying to remember the course of events, those thoughts and opinions gradually became somewhat different. And only right at the end did the term 'Room 101' occur to me, but when it did, I thought – "You know what, that is a really good metaphor for what I have been doing in my head, just dropping stuff in there so I don't have to face it." Probably for much of my life, but certainly where 7/7 and 21/7 were concerned. And so I missed the chance to see that I might be being affected by what I was dealing with – and the effect that might have had on Vanessa. And now, of course, it's too late to change any of that. Perhaps there's a useful lesson in there for others who might find themselves in similar situations at some point in their lives.

Anyway, now it's written. Of course, it is now several years since all this happened, and although I had a few notes, basically this is all from memory – so it is bound to be flawed and hazy, certainly not an accurate chronicle. And I will say this here – I think I did an OK job with it all, but only because of everyone else who contributed – but I believe that the whole 7/7 and 21/7 thing was the main reason for my OBE, though I can't ever know for sure. Bottom line, I don't think that my contribution was even close to meriting the OBE, but I was only too happy to accept it – for Vanessa's sake, for all she'd had to put up with; late-night calls, disappearing off to places at short notice, generally not being around much, and for all my own faults. And then she was so proud, and she gets a day at the Palace, and she loved that all. So as far as I'm concerned, the OBE was hers. Anyway – the story…

7 JULY 2005

First, a quick explanation of where I worked at the time. This is an establishment known as the Forensic Explosives Laboratory (FEL). The function of the FEL is to provide police forces with a forensic investigation service into the explosives aspects of any incidents of the criminal misuse of explosives on the UK mainland. The FEL is based on a Ministry of Defence (MOD) site at Fort Halstead, near Sevenoaks in Kent. Hereinafter, this establishment is referred to as either the Fort or FEL, which I have used interchangeably. The part of the MOD that this site is used by is the Defence Science and Technology Laboratory, otherwise known as Dstl, and FEL is part of this larger organisation. The main point to note here is that, although FEL's work is largely for the police, rather than the MOD, and is hence generally quite self-contained within Dstl, FEL does, on occasion, need access to the wider facilities of Dstl, and this will become apparent later in this narrative.

Sat at my desk, maybe 08.30, quite early for me, can't remember why, but that was about to change (along with many other things, though I knew nothing of that just then). The phone rings. It's Geoff (FEL's police liaison officer), says there's reports of an incident on the Tube, Piccadilly line, Russell Square. They're not sure what, calling it a 'power outage', but just a heads up at the moment. So I wander down to the liaison office for a chat. What's a 'power outage' then? No one's sure but Geoff's got the news on now. And something certainly seems to be happening, and some first reports that there may be some casualties. From a power outage? Gradually it becomes clear that whatever it is, something quite bad has happened and SO15 (the Met police anti-terrorist branch, SO13 as they were then, but SO15 now) are attending.

So I wander round to Kim's office, give her a heads up that she may need to attend a scene, but not sure at the moment. Also suggested that if there is something, it may be good for Richard to go along, he's not been to a scene before. In hindsight, maybe I wouldn't have suggested that, but I had no clue at that point how the day (and in a way my life) was going to unfold.

Well, things accelerated pretty quickly from there, with more reports of similar incidents at Aldgate and Edgware stations. 'Power outage' wasn't cutting it any longer. As luck would have it Sarah L was staying in her flat near Canary Wharf at the time, and she hadn't left for FEL, having heard about problems on the Tube, and she phoned in, so I asked her if she was OK to go straight to Aldgate and offer her services to whoever was there for SO15 – which of course she was.

Meanwhile, Kim and Richard arrived at the RVP (rendezvous point) for Russell Square – by which time a bus had blown up in Tavistock Square, so SO15 asked Kim to go there, and leave poor Richard at Russell Square – some introduction to a scene! Indeed, given the growing realisation that some kind of multiple attack on London was in progress, Richard being only an assistant case officer, should not and could not be left at that scene by himself.

Which still left Edgware Station, so Hazel was despatched there. Claire was on leave, and Sharon was somewhere else, for the morning at least, so that left only me to go and rescue Richard. So a police car was summoned to the Fort – but by then management were beginning to stir themselves, and asking about – guess what – health and safety, have to have someone from SHEF (Safety, Health, Environment and Fire, our health and safety department)! Well as it happened, my brother Rob was working in SHEF for Dstl at the time, so I said OK, if I must have someone, I'll take him. Later, there were mutterings that I should have taken Charlie from SHEF, because he was more senior. I won't get into all that here (that could be its own chapter!). Suffice it to say, I simply said that Charlie's safety expertise is with explosives – I don't need that, *I* am one of Dstl's top explosives experts, especially with IEDs (Improvised Explosive Devices). If I need any safety advice, it's for all the rest (structures, noxious fumes, dust, asbestos, etc.), so if I must take someone (this need to have someone from SHEF never ever happened before or after this day!) then Rob was it. And he was very useful, for many reasons, but not least because he could deal with risk assessments, for Russell Square and the other scenes, and I could concentrate on the reason FEL was actually there, which was to help the police work out what had happened, and provide information to help with investigative leads.

So that's it, all available people were now deployed from the lab (and pretty much from SO15 I think). Fortunately there were no more scenes – just then at any rate. By now the powers that be were approaching controlled panic mode – the London public transport system was shut down, the rescue/paramedic services were now at full stretch, and still no one really knew what had happened, beyond some kind of probable bomb attacks – but most particularly, if the perpetrators were still out there. Were there more to come? If so, what should they be looking for?

Rob and I arrived at Russell Square, courtesy of a police car from the Fort, at around midday, and found the RV point – a proper SO15 wagon by then. There we were told that Richard and the SO15 scene manager (Robin) had gone down to the train, along with the EXPO and maybe some others. (An EXPO is a Metropolitan Police Explosives Officer – the Met has its own bomb disposal teams, all ex-military EOD [Explosive Ordnance Disposal] officers. Military EOD teams are used for the rest of the country.) This was precisely what I had wanted to avoid – Richard being dragged down there on his own. So I said that Rob and I had to go and join them, which after some debate, we were allowed to do. We were escorted into the station, down in the lift (no escalators there), and along to the end of the platform, where the tunnel starts. Here I couldn't help noticing a lot of discarded paramedic type materials, empty wrappers, IV bottles and such like, spread around the platform end. Presumably where some people had been treated, under better conditions than just in the tunnel on the tracks. Though how they had got there if they couldn't walk wasn't immediately apparent – there was no sign of any train in the tunnel as far as we could see down it, so quite a carrying operation then, if that had been required? Anyway – this was the point at which our escort stopped, and said we would have to walk along the track through the tunnel from there – a few hundred metres he thought! Hmm, OK then – having been assured that the power was definitely off to the tracks and would definitely not be coming back on anytime soon! So off we set, avoiding the conductor rail assiduously, despite being assured it was off – we both felt disinclined to test it!

We must have had a torch, though I don't fully recall that, but we had gone maybe 100 metres, and could see that the tunnel curved, when we both heard a rumbling that seemed to come from up ahead. Which there should definitely not be! The whole system was shut down. We *knew* this. Some kind of tunnel echo effect? So we carried on a bit but it started getting louder – and we could now feel the track rails vibrating. And this is a very small tunnel, there is no more than maybe six inches in places, between the train and the walls. My memory may be hazy now, but on this it is still pin sharp. We *knew* there could not be a train coming – there was a train stuck in the tunnel for God's sake – but we also knew what our senses were telling us (somewhere between WTF and aaarrgh!). To hell with this, we now went straight for a nook in the side of the tunnel, which there were at intervals along the way, and waited. Sure enough, the noise got louder, and then there was a light, visible and growing, coming from around the curve! And something did come round the corner – a sort of small, open cart, running on the rails, with a number of people standing up in it.

It turns out that London Transport and the fire brigade, between them, had come up with this idea of a mobile rail cart with an electric motor, that could be taken apart and carried on a rescue wagon and assembled on the tracks, for moving people and equipment for just such an occasion as this. Only no one had told us that before sending us off down the tunnel!

So we started waving our torch at the approaching trolley (which was also something of a surprise to them), but as they came up to us I could see Richard and the EXPO amongst sundry others. It transpired they were finished with an initial look at the scene, now that all the living casualties had been removed, and were heading back up to plan the next moves. Very generously, they offered us a lift back the way we had come – duly accepted.

Now this was a new and really quite weird experience for me, which is quite hard to explain. Oh, the basics are simple enough, just as described above. But the sensations at the time were… well, weird. It was sort of like watching a good illusion in a magic show, except that this was real, and with the potential to be squished between a Tube train and a wall – while at the same time *sort of* knowing that that *can't* happen. Scary? Well a bit maybe, but then again not very. Just – weird. And in terms of new experiences, just one of some much, much worse to come.

As everyone reconvened at the SO15 RVP wagon, rather than the pace of events ramping up, as you might expect, in fact the opposite happened – everything gradually ground to a halt. All the living casualties had been removed, but now there was a jurisdictional dispute, at least partly as I recall, to do with disaster victim recovery teams versus crime scene integrity/recovery teams. And indeed, some still not entirely resolved explosives safety questions, though the EXPO was *reasonably* happy that there were no more explosive devices or materials in a detonable state.

However, lulls like this are not uncommon at large bomb scenes, and it gave me a chance to get my own thoughts together, from an FEL point of view, and catch up with what was happening with Kim, Hazel and Sarah at the other scenes, and coordinate all that with those back at the lab. Though one of the things I do remember was that the mobile phone networks were struggling, or even maybe switched off for some of the time, which later led to FEL getting some emergency service type sims for our work phones.

My first concern, however, was Richard. I think he had probably been OK until he had actually gone down to the scene with the police, which I had really wanted to avoid, but had got there just too late. Of course, he could have just refused to do so until I got there (he knew I was on the way), but that would have been difficult to do with the pressure from the police to get things underway. From their point of view, they wanted an FEL person, and he was who they had, so they would just go with that. Understandable from their perspective, and under the circumstances he did as well as he could possibly have been expected to. But it seemed to me he was (entirely understandably) somewhat overwhelmed by the whole episode. So I got him to go through with me what he had seen, and what it might have meant, wrote my notes about that, and then told him to go straight home, via the lab if necessary (to get his car, etc.), but not to stay or do anything else there – he was done for the day.

I think Sharon must have just had the day off, because by this time contact had been made with her, and she had said she would be able to come to the scene – I didn't want to have an individual case myself, I would need to be coordinating the whole FEL response. It was already clear that this was going to be the biggest operation ever dealt with by the FEL, with multiple, coordinated and deliberate mass casualty scenes. As it turned out, Sarah M was also available at this point so Sharon would bring her as an assistant.

Probably around 3–4 pm now, and the waiting was starting to drag a bit. The arguments were growing about the next step – were SO15 evidence recovery in charge or disaster victim recovery (DVR) in charge? This was entirely a police matter, though I was firmly in the SO15 camp. And Robin was doing (I thought) a great job of fighting his corner. I hadn't worked with him before, so I was unaware of his fiery reputation, but I was about to find out. Robin was a DS (detective sergeant). Keep that in mind, because at that moment a superintendent from DVR came into the RV wagon, asking for the scene manager – Robin. This superintendent wanted Robin to take him into the scene so that he could start to organise the DVR process. Robin politely declined, saying that, until he was told otherwise by his management, his job was to manage the scene and organise evidence recovery, now that the living casualties had been removed. The superintendent became more insistent – and so did Robin. And so the conversation deteriorated, with the superintendent starting to pull rank, but with no discernible effect on Robin! It finally culminated in the superintendent directly ordering Robin to do as he was told – to be advised by Robin that he didn't care if he was the Queen of fucking Sheba, he wasn't going into the fucking scene, and to fuck off out of his RV wagon! To which I thought – Bravo!

Well, with almost perfect timing, perhaps a minute later, the phone rang in the wagon, which Robin answered. It was Robin's boss, an SO15 DI (detective inspector), saying, "Just a heads up, Robin, I've sent a DVR superintendent down to see you, while this is all sorted out. Keep him sweet, will you?" At which point I had to leave the wagon, as howling with laughter would have seemed insensitive!

I later learned that this incident was treated by Robin's boss with a sort of resigned sigh, as Robin was quite well known for this approach, and the DVR guy was just another victim, and no one to lose any sleep over. Apart from which, everyone was naturally very stressed, and had far more important things to worry about just then – probably just as well for Robin, since in a different situation, this probably would have been a big deal.

Eventually the impasse was sorted, with SO15 having primacy, but agreeing to allow the removal of the bodies as a priority, where it would not significantly interfere with essential evidence recovery. As a later learning point, SO15 exhibits officers were all to be trained in DV recovery protocols, so as to be able to incorporate that into their whole scene management approach.

In fact, although frustrating at the time, this delay worked out, because Sharon arrived with Sarah M at about 17.00, and without the delay they would have been too late to go down with Robin and Co., for the first evidence recovery phase.

And so, back down into the tunnel, me, Rob, Sharon, Sarah, Robin and I'm sure one or two others, this time by means of the motorised trolley, which was a much better means of travelling than trying to walk along the tunnel.

As we approached the front of the train and came to a stop, we saw the first hints of the nightmare that awaited, and the nightmare that must have been faced by victims and rescue workers alike – discarded medical wrappers and IV bottles, etc., discarded around the track in front of the train. These would have been from casualties taken out of the carriage and then treated on the track (or maybe the trolley) – but in either case, the horror of the dark and dirt and confusion of trying to do that can only be imagined. The train had just passed through a wider tunnel junction and then entered this narrow tunnel when it came to a stop. Here there is only inches between the train and tunnel walls, but these trains have a door in the front of the driver's cab, presumably with this in mind, and this is how we now entered the train. And here the nightmare proper started.

The driver's cab was relatively undamaged, but through that into the carriage proper, the true scale of the horror became apparent. The floor of the aisle between the seats was passable with care, but was slick with blood and human remains. Bodies and larger human remains were piled all along the seats on either side, with little yellow signs saying 'DEAD' on most of the recognisably human ones. Up to the first set of doors (I think they were still present though damaged), and on along the aisle, more bodies piled on seats, more yellow signs, and the floor getting more difficult to walk on – with no handrails, etc. to hold on to, all being missing or detached by the blast. And so up to the second set of doors – all of which were missing, blown out onto the track where the tunnel widened out into the underground junction, a little further down the train. The blast had happened in the wider part, before the train came to a halt with the first carriage now into the narrow tunnel. All of the train windows were missing, blown out with the explosion, and at the standing area where the doors had been, there was clearly a depression in the floor of the train – except that it was approximately flat with the remaining floor, being full of more or less compacted apparent human remains (much as Richard had described to me earlier). Which made it hard to tell how big or deep it was, and walking around it was an exercise in not slipping over, with not much to hold onto, all the handrails missing or detached as described above. The aisle on the other side of this second standing area was much the same, slippery underfoot, with more bodies and more yellow stickers piled up along both sides, up to the end door of the carriage into the next one along.

Not much further along the train (maybe the second carriage?), where the tunnel was much wider, and other tracks merged, access was available into the train from the side doors. Beyond the first carriage, the train was pretty much intact, with no more bodies or obvious human remains, although there was certainly more evidence of paramedic activity. The doors were all open now, allowing access out onto the track, where the first carriage had been when the blast occurred.

And so out onto the tracks, now in the wide part of the tunnel, where other tracks met and went off down other tunnels. First we got out on the wide side, where the other tracks were, though it was also possible to get out on the other side, where the tunnel wall was, which was now further away from the side of the train. We would come back to that. So, on the tracks side, as we got out we saw quite a bit of debris, including the doors – and more bodies, perhaps three or four. Clearly this was where the front carriage had been when the blast occurred, and, as the bomb had been in the standing area, by the doors, when the doors had blown out, so had some of the passengers who had been standing there. As I recall, these bodies showed mostly very similar damage to those inside the carriage, in particular traumatic amputations to the lower limbs. Although in no way a medical assessment, observing injuries to bodies close to an explosion can give important information in an explosives context, with high explosives causing recognisable and specific injuries to bodies, including traumatic amputation of limbs, generally with charring of the flesh close to where the amputations occur. And this damage generally only occurs when a body is close to the explosive when it detonates, really only within a very few feet, depending on the size of the charge. So these people had been very close to the explosion, and it appeared to have been at or around floor level.

Now we re-entered the carriage, and went out down on the other side of the train, next to the tunnel wall. And along here was perhaps, for me anyway, the most difficult sight of all. So far, most of the dead had been close to the blast, and were severely damaged, as already described. In addition to the bodily injuries, again when very close to a high explosive blast, clothing tends to be also very badly damaged, both torn/shredded but also charred and sooted. So as cold as it sounds, I was able to focus on them all as 'bodies' rather than people, and keep my concentration on what I needed to be looking for in terms of information useful to the police, and not be distracted by the human devastation I was seeing. I was also very conscious of needing to stay calm for Sharon and Sarah, and indeed Rob, and make sure they were managing OK and not, for instance, being overwhelmed and needing to go back up to the street. This could very easily have been the case for any of us, and cause for absolutely no criticism whatsoever. But so far, so good, and we all seemed to be coping.

And then Sharon and I (I don't think Sarah, maybe she didn't get out with us on this side) came upon a new sight. A man was almost neatly wrapped around one of the train wheels, but in this case he was, at first sight, completely intact, along with the clothes he was wearing – a light blue suit as I recall. And now this was very hard to look at, because he was so clearly a real person, who had, if possible, an even more horrific end than some of the others, for many of whom at least, death would have been, if not instantaneous, then at least very quick. This person must have been standing on the other side of the standing area, against the doors, with a number of people between him and the bomb, so he would have been shielded quite effectively from the immediate blast. But then when the doors went out, he had clearly been pushed out with them, most likely still fully conscious, and relatively uninjured. He had then fallen to the track and was ultimately caught up in a train wheel and rolled around it as the train stopped. I remember thinking his head looked a slightly strange shape, but otherwise he looked outwardly quite undamaged.

This image will stay with me forever, but around that, mercifully, I am quite hazy. I'm fairly sure I said something to Sharon along the lines of, "He's clearly not explosively damaged, we'll just note that, and where he is, and move right along" – i.e. back into the carriage and the slightly more tolerable carnage.

I'm also fairly sure that we took one or more explosive testing kits down with us, which we used on some parts of the inside of the carriage, although that was always going to be a forlorn hope, since blood and human tissue will fairly comprehensively mask or degrade small explosives traces. But still it needed to be done, so we looked for the cleanest surfaces we could find, close to the seat of the explosion and swabbed there, for later examination at the lab. We may also have swabbed the detached doors, though I can't remember for sure. It seems to me (now at least) that that would have been a good place to swab, though in the end it wouldn't have mattered anyway, given the nature of the explosive it later transpired was used – but we knew nothing of that at the time.

And then, having got some samples, and a fairly clear picture of what we had to deal with, we all headed back to the surface, to take stock, and decide how to proceed from there.

Here seems like a good place for some musings on dealing with something like this, I mean on an emotional level, not in a forensic context. Now it may be thought that, working in the forensic explosives field, such a scene was not a new experience for me – indeed my department head even made a comment along those lines to me, when he saw me a day or two later! It was meant in the best way, but still, it showed either a lack of understanding of how bad these scenes really were, or of what the work of an explosives forensic scientist (in the UK at any rate), was generally like (or probably a bit of both). But within my twenty years to that point, mass casualty bombings of civilians had never occurred on the UK mainland. Certainly, I had encountered dead bodies, some explosively damaged, but I had never experienced anything even approaching this scene.

Now some organisations, certainly today, would automatically require their staff exposed to something like this, to attend counselling afterwards, but that was less so at the time, and certainly wasn't the case for Dstl. So do I think that should be/ should have been the case? If it's automatic, then probably I would say no – people are all different, there is no one solution for everyone. It's a very complex matter and one issue, among many, is timing. People's reactions can be very different, and particularly they can occur at very different times after such an event, so simply saying "you've seen this, now go have some counselling", is probably not a very effective approach. However, such support should certainly be offered, but more on the basis of if or when an individual feels they need it, and for an indefinite period into the future, which could even be years. Of course, the trouble with this is that (a) you might not realise until damage is done, that you do need some help; and (b) you might feel some stigma attached to asking for help. So, as well as the offer of help, there needs to be some system of watching out for possible signs of issues arising amongst those potentially affected.

As I said, Dstl had no system of any kind in place at the time, although it was made clear to everyone that help could be provided through occupational health at any time, if anyone should request it. However, it seemed to me that the best help at the time was for people to just sit and talk about it with each other as and when they wished. I did make a point of watching out for signs of any trouble for a while afterwards, particularly for Richard, who I thought at the time showed that he might have been the most affected. Though what do I know? That may just indicate that he had a more healthy reaction to it all than the rest of us! At any rate, I am unaware of anyone suffering any significant after-effects from these scenes – and thank God for that.

Personally? My approach was to largely just put it out of my mind and concentrate on the job in hand. One thing I did notice was that, in the days that followed, naturally the papers were full of what had happened, and much of that was the human stories of the many people who had been there, and I consciously avoided any and all such articles and pictures. Really an extension of what I was doing in the tunnel, keeping it all as just 'people', and staying away from thinking in terms of the victims as actual individuals with lives and families and all the rest. And pretty much this seemed to work for me. Well, so far so good anyway. One thing I do now entirely understand is how, for instance, many soldiers will not talk about bad things they have seen with their families and loved ones, even when exhorted to do so. The fact is, that faced with something that bad, the very last people you want to talk to about it, are those you love most – simply because it *is* so awful; the last thing you want to do is put any of that on them. So I go back to what I said above – if talking is necessary, and I'm sure that it mostly is a beneficial thing to do at some point – then it should be to someone, or a group, who was either there with you, or at least has experienced something similar.

So – back out of the tunnel, to the SO15 wagon. "OK, now you've seen it – what can you tell us, Cliff!?" Crunch time. And in my head I'm thinking, "Erm, well, looks like a bomb has gone off down there." Still in protective, 'don't think about the human horror' mode, but the time for any kind of levity, no matter what the reason, was long since past. Giving myself a moment to focus, I gave my opinion that several kilograms of a high explosive had detonated, at or about floor level in the standing area of the second set of doors in from the front of the first carriage. So far, so uncontroversial, and still not especially helpful for the police, for whom the burning question was – was this a suicide bombing, or has someone left a device and is out there maybe getting ready to set another one?

It may seem that my answer thus far was, in practice, no different to that first thought in my head as above. But, getting technical for a minute, that's actually not true. I was saying it's a *high* explosive – that means it needs a detonator to make it work. Detonators are hard to come by in the UK even more so than high explosives. It also means that it was not any kind of pressure device, not a pipe bomb, not a pressure cooker or anything similar, and not any kind of pyrotechnic (i.e. firework) type of main charge – which are a class of materials known as *low* explosives. So it did give the police some information, just not the really crucial bit that they wanted right then.

Now, with my fingers and all other available appendages firmly crossed, I said my best opinion at that time was that it probably was a suicide bomber, then hurriedly added all the usual good forensic science caveats. Knowing full well that at that moment, such caveats would be politely received and then quickly filed under 'never mind all that'. A stretch though it was, this opinion was not entirely unfounded. In particular, there was one body I had noted that seemed particularly badly damaged. Most of the bodies had severe trauma, and traumatic amputations to their lower bodies, also to the lower trunk, but facially they had been largely intact. Whereas, this one body seemed to have suffered more damage to the trunk, but also had pretty much no face left. Unfortunately, as a necessary consequence of the rescue operation, bodies and materials had been moved around to provide access, and this also meant that their position thereafter, could not be used to help work out the actual sequence of events. Clearly, I had not examined, or even properly seen, all the bodies that were there, but still, this one had stood out to me. I was confident that the device had been at floor level (i.e. not being carried at chest or back height), and I could see this kind of damage being sustained if someone was crouching down next to it, perhaps to trigger it.

And so, on that limited basis I gave my opinion. Fortunately it turned out to be correct, though clearly the police were still alive to the possibility that there were still others out there, intent on doing something similar.

I also talked to Hazel and Sarah L at the other Tube scenes, and Kim at the bus. I can't remember if any of them felt able to give opinions about suicide bombers at that point, but they were clearly similar types of devices, and nothing to argue against the suicide scenario, so I think the working assumption by the police by then was that they were all suicide bombs.

By this time, it was somewhere around midnight, so I thought it was probably time we headed home. Umm... well now, it's all very well (and speaking personally, quite fun) getting a fast police ride to a scene, but then comes the question – how do you get back home!? The police are very good at getting you somewhere *they* want you to be. But taking you back, well that just isn't a priority! And to be fair the whole force was quite preoccupied at that point. And clearly there was no public transport. OK, yes they would get us a ride back – but it might take a while. I can remember sitting with Sharon on some steps to a building near the Tube entrance, just waiting. I remember just chatting, which seems quite banal considering the enormity of what we had spent the day dealing with, but probably the best way of coping, at least at that time. I can't actually remember if Rob or Sarah were also there then – maybe they were, but also maybe they had got a ride back earlier. I could check, but that's not the point of this article – and an interesting example (to me anyway) of the vagaries of human memory in general, and mine in particular. Anyway, I think we eventually got a ride at about 01.30, so I probably actually got home about 03.00.

And that was the start of my new regime – for perhaps the next four months, even on the relatively normal days, I was getting into work about 07.30 or earlier. Absolutely out of necessity, both from what had just happened and from what was still to come, but thereafter it sort of became a bit ingrained. Looking back on it now, I wonder if that was an indication that I had changed a bit, not just from this one day but from the whole of the next few months, which was certainly very – um… *intense* is the best way I can think to describe it. I'm sure it was very hard on Vanessa, certainly for those few months; it screwed up our plans for the summer, she was still recovering from her cancer treatment, and I was effectively gone for most of the time – even when I was physically present, I think I was probably absent mentally for a lot of the time. She was a rock for me throughout, and I certainly wouldn't have got through it without her. Actually – this is suddenly very difficult – I don't think I've ever consciously thought about this before. How crazy is that!? When I've thought about that time at all, it's always just been along the lines of, "Well that's lucky, I have never really been affected by those events at all." But now – well maybe I changed more than I knew. Not in any of the common, obvious ways like having flashbacks or nightmares, or being angry or depressed, but… well, I've always been a bit more introvert than extrovert, so maybe I just became more so than I was before. Which would not be a good thing. All far too late now, and the one person who could maybe tell me is no longer here to ask. And maybe she did tell me, or try to. I'll never know.

Well. This is an unexpected outcome, and not the original idea for writing this at all. And that being so, I'm going to just leave this hook alone here, and maybe come back to it later…

And while on the subject of being supported, I will say now for the record, that all of the FEL people who were involved in this performed wonderfully, both individually and together as a team, and I am eternally grateful to them all for that. Without their wholehearted support, I'm sure I would have simply crashed and burned.

8–11 JULY

Intense activity within the lab and back at the scenes. What was the explosive? What was it carried in? Was there anything in the debris to help the police identify the perpetrators? As the bodies and human remains were removed from the carriages, the damage and loose debris could be more closely examined. And then there was the question of how to move the carriages from where they were – and where to take them so they could be examined in detail in a controlled environment. Now SO15 always loved a challenge, and could make a competition out of anything. Generally, all debris and movable items from a scene would be brought to FEL for examination – we had a lot of space and some pretty big buildings. The biggest single item we had had before was a double-decker bus, and in fact the only thing not brought to us before, was the Lockerbie aircraft debris – that really was too big, and anyway was not our expertise to deal with. It was eventually all taken to the AAIB premises at Farnborough where it was partially reconstructed.

Anyway, the competition now was to see if they could transport the Tube carriages to FEL, since that would clearly break all previous records. To which my response was my version of a John McEnroe type 'you can *not* be serious!' Well they were – but eventually wiser heads (and more pertinently, practical logistics!) ruled, and they were taken to some railway sheds in Acton, where they stayed for several weeks, maybe even months. There they had all the facilities and tools for proper detailed examinations, inside, outside and underneath, and FEL staff got to know those sheds quite well over the next few weeks. The bus however did come to FEL – we did have the space and facilities for that, so at least SO15 could claim to have matched the previous record!

12 JULY

Things really kicked off again for the lab on this day, when a number of strands of the ongoing police investigation came together, with the finding of a car full of explosive devices at Luton train station, and a premises in Leeds which turned out to be the main bomb-making factory for the bombers. Not that we had been far short of flat out on our various examinations and analyses, but this really stepped it up a gear. Up until now we had been really struggling to find out what explosives had been used and how the devices had been constructed. None of our preliminary tests was coming up positive, which was starting to cause some head scratching, as we would normally have expected to have found at least some indication of what explosive had been used by this time.

Now we had some potential unused materials in a car, and maybe the main bomb factory, which would be a major step forward for us in understanding what we were dealing with.

Most of the lab staff were still working flat out at the various scenes, or in the lab on stuff from those scenes but Claire and Sarah M were available – so they were whisked off to Leeds by helicopter, as that seemed like the bigger, more complicated scene. Now it has to be said that being transported around by helicopter was a fairly rare occurrence, so this was a good example of the state of mind of the powers that be, at that time. Basically, anything the police wanted, they could have, where and when they wanted it.

Which really left only me for the Luton car – which given

all the various strands going on at the time, I didn't especially want to go to. However, that was all still being dealt with by the EXPO, so maybe I could just discuss it with him on the phone. Which is what we did, and we came up with a plan for how he could get me a sample of some of the materials he had found, and then make safe and/or destroy the rest of what he had there.

Now, from my chat with him, it was clear that what he was very likely dealing with, at least in part, were some very dangerous materials and complete IEDs, so the safest option, for him, would have been to simply do remotely what the press like to call a 'controlled explosion'. This, however, would risk losing us the chance of a sample of unused explosive, which we had been struggling to identify. So when he said he was happy to get me an actual sample first, this was a very brave decision for him to take, irrespective of having discussed how he might do it. So I was at pains to point out – it was absolutely his decision, and we would work with whatever he got us, and never EVER question what he chose to do. But get an actual sample he did. Which turned out to be HMTD (hexamethylene-triperoxide-diamine), which is a very sensitive and dangerous high explosive, that can be used as an explosive in its own right, but more sensibly is used in small quantities to detonate a much larger amount of much less sensitive explosive.

This was a big step forward for the lab as now we had a clear direction and focus for at least some of what we should be looking for.

12–14 JULY – LEEDS

Meanwhile, Claire and Sarah M had arrived at the premises in Leeds. And here things weren't going quite so well. One of the reasons the Met have their own EXPOs is that they are only a small team, and they get to choose the best people available, and they have all already had full careers in the military, with a great deal of experience. The military EOD organisation is much bigger, and necessarily has a whole range of staff, from newly qualified to nearing retirement – meaning a whole range of experience.

Well, as it happened, the EOD officer sent to the Leeds premises was at the younger and less experienced end of the spectrum. Don't get me wrong, they are all properly qualified in terms of actual bomb disposal. Which would have been fine if this was a normal EOD type of incident, with one or more actual devices to deal with. However, this scene was anything but.

So, he had followed his procedures, gone in for an initial safety inspection, looking for any actual devices and/or booby traps – and found, at first sight, nothing of the sort. What he found was best described as a complete shithole, with apparent rubbish (screwed up papers, dirty dishes, plastic trays, buckets of various sorts of slop, including buckets of very smelly dark brown stuff – believed by him and several others after him to be actual shit), being spread liberally over the floors (and every other flat surface including chairs) throughout the flat. To the point that there was very little clear floor space left to actually walk on. There were also several rubber gloves, dust masks, and much more worryingly, proper gas masks. Well you had to feel for him, but this was something he really didn't understand, or think it was something he was best placed to deal with.

Which didn't help Claire or Sarah – they couldn't enter until he declared the scene explosively safe, which he couldn't, because he didn't understand what he was seeing. To be fair to him, he was happy to get Claire and Sarah some samples from within, which they tested with the limited test kits they had available – which gave them no useful results. And so things came to a full stop. Now all that was left to do was to get some samples to the lab. Since most of the material in there was these various sludges, from light yellow to dark brown, it was decided that these were what should be sent. How to do that? By helicopter of course. Only there weren't any available just then.

Then followed a conversation between the police and the 'powers that be' that I have no knowledge of but I can imagine to be something like, "There are no helicopters." "Really?" "Yes really." "In the whole of the UK? Get a grip, there must be one somewhere!" "No. There aren't any." "Well try harder, and find one." "You're not listening, there aren't any available – well, there is the Lossiemouth search and rescue Sea King helicopter, but that is clearly out of the quest—" "Great, that'll do, get it on its way then." Amazingly that is what then happened! So Sarah was despatched back to the lab from Leeds on the Lossiemouth Sea King – no silly little police helicopter this. I heard tea and biscuits were provided, a paper to read; the full in-flight service! I later heard that the bill for this ran to six figures. No idea if that is true, but I can believe it. As I noted previously, with a government in mild panic mode, stuff that would normally be impossible, just happens. What *is* true is that Sarah can claim the most expensive journey in FEL history, which will almost certainly never be matched.

I should just add here that the samples Sarah brought back to the Fort were very small. Can you imagine the furore if a coastguard Sea King fell out of the sky due to an accident carrying some kind of unknown, novel, improvised explosive!

Anyway, now back at FEL we had some samples of yellow/brown sludge. Over the next day, a battery of tests revealed – almost nothing! At least nothing that made any sense to us. About the only things we found were that it was aqueous, it might have some peroxide in it, and apparently a bit of something called piperine. What's piperine? Good question. Consulting the books, apparently it is a constituent of some peppers, and is sometimes used in insecticides. Really no help at all in terms of explosives. Well, there were some gas masks there – could it be chemical weapon related? There's been absolutely no indication of this but we're getting nowhere, let Porton Down have a sample. Porton Down is the UK chemical and biological defence research establishment – which is also part of Dstl. So this was the substance of a conversation between me and SO15 at about 22.00; all agreed they will take some first thing in the morning to Porton Down.

So I go home, wind down, go to bed, just get to sleep – the phone rings. It's now about 01.00. A fast car is on its way to the FEL to pick up the samples and take them to Porton. If I hurry into the lab to facilitate, their engine won't get too cold waiting for me! At which point I did suffer a serious sense of humour failure. Something like "You couldn't have fucking said this earlier at 22.00, when I was still at the fucking lab!" But this was a shift change, fresh person, eager to do stuff, etc., etc. So off I trot, at 02.00 I arrive at the lab, faff around, leave at 03.00, home, wind down again, back to bed maybe 04.30. And then back to the lab for 07.30, or so. I put this in only because I actually remember this instance of briefly losing my temper; and by way of an example of the kind of fevered atmosphere that we were working in at the time, and for the next several weeks – not just me but all the FEL staff, the police, everyone. I guess it must take its toll somewhere along the way. Maybe there is something to this counselling/therapy malarkey after all. I just don't know how it would work – if I had been told to do some such thing at the time, I would have simply said something like "Oh bog off, I haven't got time for all that nonsense now."

Anyway, back to Leeds. Claire is still stuck at the premises, the EOD officer has gone, saying he can't do any more, but hasn't cleared the premises so neither Claire nor anybody else can go in. Well, now that Porton Down have become involved, they have sent a mobile laboratory up to Leeds in case it does turn out to involve some kind of chemical weapon as well. After speaking to Claire, we agree that she could stay there for a while, to liaise with Porton, and also because the police are saying they might have some other premises in the area where they might need her.

Well I can't now remember the actual sequence of events, but let's say that by the end of 16 July, Porton had come up with the same results as FEL, and had decided they could find no evidence of anything they would recognise as a chemical threat, so they decamped back to Porton Down. Of course there was still the nightmare scenario of some kind of biological device, also for Porton to decide, but to test for that, in the absence of any idea of what to look for, can take weeks and they still may not find anything. Claire had made her way back to the Fort; not sure how but certainly not by helicopter! The scene was still shut and no one could decide how to proceed, which was causing severe agitation, not least amongst the police. I think by this time we had had one sample, from amongst those collected by the EOD, in which we had found HMTD. Which was thus far the only concrete evidence of illegal activity at the scene, and linked to the actual bombers, and to their car at Luton.

Two more days passed, of agonising at senior levels within the government and police over how to proceed. This culminated in me being called to a meeting on 19 July at NSY (New Scotland Yard), with senior police, SO15 officers, and a senior scientist from Porton Down – and being told to bring an overnight bag! A proper amount of sucking of teeth and chewing of lips ensued, but it all boiled down to this: Porton Down could find no evidence of anything they could recognise as chemical, nor indeed biological weapons although that was much more nebulous, though we all understood there were no guarantees. On the other hand, there was good evidence of at least some recognisable explosives manufacture, which also linked to the bombers and the car at Luton. So, was everyone agreed that we could just treat it as an explosives scene and actually get moving again? Please? I said I was happy with that – and within five minutes I was in a police car, bag in hand and blue lights flashing, heading rapidly for Leeds.

At the same time as I was racing up the M1, EOD had been re-tasked to the scene. And this time, they sent a different EOD officer, and one at the opposite end of the experience spectrum to the earlier one, which was a real boon. Having had his own look around, he was very happy to take both me and Chris, the SO15 exhibits officer, into the premises with him. The only minor complication to that was, initially at least, we had to climb in through the living room window (this was a ground-floor flat), because that was a common procedure, which the first EOD officer had followed, when there is a danger that normal points of entry might be booby-trapped. And inside it was fairly much as it had previously been described, but now we could start to figure out just what it was that we actually had to deal with. It soon became clear that a major and quite long-term process of manufacture of a variety of materials had been taking place, and a large part seemed to be various mixtures containing black pepper and hydrogen peroxide. Nothing like anything we had ever seen or even heard of before – could they possibly become explosive? Chemically speaking, it was theoretically possible, but that's a long way from saying it could work in practice. All of which, I think, was quite frustrating for the police (and actually for us), but the police were not used to us having to say things like, "Erm, sorry, I'm not sure – it might be that."

A bit of light relief in all this, was the buckets with the very dark brown stuff that looked, and apparently smelled, like shit. Now, I don't have a sense of smell, never have had, which gave me a slightly different perspective here. Everyone else was fairly sure it was actual shit. But I didn't quite believe it – so this became a bit of a light-hearted challenge to work out who was right; there might even have been mention of a small bet. My trump card was noticing something no one else had – this was the middle of a hot July, in what was certainly a metaphorical shithole – and not a single fly. Not one. With a couple of buckets of actual shit? Not possible. And so it eventually proved! It turns out they were just mixtures of black pepper and water – no hydrogen peroxide at all. All the other mixtures contained various strengths of hydrogen peroxide. Never worked out the reason for these water mixtures, not for sure, but that's by the way.

Anyway, now we could make real progress, and over the next two days we systematically removed all the actual and potential explosive material (of which there was quite a lot) from the premises, and either packaged it for transport to the Fort, or destroyed it at the scene. Which was also where I had one of the few real "Oh shit, what the fuck are you doing, Cliff?" moments of my twenty-six years with FEL.

The biggest danger in the flat, it transpired, was the presence of, overall, probably a few hundred grams of HMTD. Fortunately though, it was not all together in one place but spread around in much smaller quantities in plastic trays and on filter papers, etc. I was confident it was HMTD from our earlier tests at FEL, and because I had done a burn test on a few very small samples on the tip of a small spatula, which had all given an immediate bright orange flash, with a satisfying little whuumph. So after taking a few very small samples for the lab, we had a plan to dispose of it, bit by bit, using a 'killer' solution, and then putting all the residues and contaminated papers, etc., into a wonderful little 'igloo' of sandbags, built by the EOD officer for this purpose, which would be closed up and the contents ignited remotely, once we had finished. The thing is, the 'killer' is only partially effective, particularly with more than just very small amounts, so we were also keeping the contents damp with an alcohol/water solution as we were going along. This would tend to keep any live material less sensitive than if it was allowed to dry out. All very well. But it was a particularly hot and sunny spell of weather. And there came a point near the end of the process, when I was on my hands and knees, with my head stuck inside the igloo, adding some more stuff to the pile. Just at that point the sun was shining directly over my shoulder and into the igloo, and as I lifted my head I suddenly noticed all these little motes of dust (almost certainly HMTD – did I say it is very sensitive?) floating and glistening in the sunlight. What with the temperature, and then the direct sunlight, despite us having tried to keep it damp, the contents had dried out nicely, and here it was warming happily in the sun – with my head stuck right in amongst it. A very bad place to be! Very gingerly, crawling backwards, and I have to say very shamefaced, I put a *lot* more damping solution in there and then suggested we put up a screen so that the sun couldn't shine straight in onto the contents. All of which I should have made sure of before. I think the expression on my face on backing out of the igloo gave the EOD officer the best laugh he'd had all day – which was actually just what we all needed. I can't remember his name now, but all respect to him – he was a top man, and his approach to everything we had to do made the whole process so much easier than it otherwise would have been.

It is now some time on 21 July. I think we were just tidying up, ready for remotely igniting the igloo contents. And by the way, when I say tidying up, this does not mean the scene was finished with, à la TV *CSI*-type programmes. All we had done was remove all the potentially explosive materials, which meant that the police no longer needed FEL or EOD to be there. And most importantly, all the people in the adjacent flats, who had been moved out when the flat was found on the 12th, could finally be allowed back into their properties. Chris and sundry other police still had several more weeks there, meticulously removing everything and anything that might possibly have some evidential or intelligence value.

At any rate we were all together in our, for want of a better word, control tent (tables, chairs, water heater, etc.), when the news came on the radio, which we just happened to have in there. And the situation we had had for the last two weeks, which you couldn't possibly imagine ever being more fraught, was about to become exactly that.

21 JULY

There it was – a perfectly calm voice on the radio, announcing that there appeared to have been another attack on the London Underground – it was thought three stations and a bus, but details were still lacking – stay tuned for further updates…

This bit I remember clearly – there was just silence for a few moments. The EOD guy was the first to speak: "Right, well that's it then – the gloves have got to come off now!" A proper military response, from a proper soldier, and whatever you might think in a comfortable debate somewhere else, at that time and in that place, we all heartily endorsed the sentiment.

Shortly thereafter, everyone's phone started ringing and plans were being rapidly remade. I stayed long enough to see the EOD officer successfully ignite his igloo contents – success being defined by the igloo remaining intact and not erupting skywards! And, as intended, by getting a good fire going in there. So that particular job was done.

Not long after that, I was heading at some speed back down the M1, with one of the SO15 officers who had been located with the Leeds police to liaise between them and NSY on the 7/7 investigation. He had been recalled for these new incidents, and it was suggested politely that I go with him. Not that I had any issue with that.

I remember getting back into London, but strangely I can't remember exactly what happened there – I think I was dropped off at Charing Cross, to make my way home from there, this being now early evening I think. Anyway, back home, and the phone was really going into overdrive now. It was now clear that all of the devices had only partially functioned and that, thereby, there were no casualties, though certainly very many badly frightened passengers.

You might think that because the devices didn't function properly, that the scenes were therefore very straightforward to deal with, but that turned out not to be the case at all. Certainly, and very thankfully, everyone was spared the horror of the 7/7 scenes, but now we had a whole new problem. The main charges had not detonated, and so they were deposited out of the rucksacks they were being carried in, onto the floor of the trains (and bus). If it had been something that we recognised or understood then that would have been OK. But this was something we had never seen before – a yellow, glutinous mess, visually fairly similar (though not quite the same) as we had seen in the bomb factory in Leeds. And that material had very clearly detonated, so we had to proceed very carefully here, especially as we still had only a vague idea of what it was – some kind of mixture of hydrogen peroxide with an organic fuel, possibly pepper. Eventually, a plan for collecting the material was formed between the EXPOs and FEL staff, whereby it would be scooped carefully from where it was into large plastic boxes, lined with large, antistatic plastic bags. The actual scooping preferably being done (I said) by the EXPOs, with the police and FEL staff watching from a safe distance – though I'm not sure that it wasn't actually a joint effort. This was all being coordinated with me, by phone, in between calls from senior police asking me how long before they could open up the Tube stations again.

And then, just as we thought we had a plan, things started going rapidly downhill. At Shepherd's Bush, Warren Street, and the bus in Hackney, as soon as they started trying to move the yellow material it suddenly started getting very hot and smoking! Now, bearing in mind that this stuff was apparently the main charge in an explosive device, this was very alarming behaviour, and naturally and sensibly, everyone immediately backed off – and all work stopped again! This is now late evening – and I'm back on the phone again. The one place this behaviour hadn't (so far) happened was at the Oval Station, but on account of it happening at the other scenes, those at the Oval were told to stop as well.

So, what do we do now – Cliff? Well, how the hell do I know? I don't even know exactly what it is, and even if I knew the exact mix, I would still have only the vaguest notion of its properties! But then, no one else would know either. I knew nothing remotely like this had ever been seen in the UK before and, as it later transpired, nowhere else in the world either. But anyway, at that moment it wasn't the rest of the world's problem, it was the UK's – and now specifically mine! OK – well give it an hour to cool, try once more very gently, see if it has finished reacting. Maybe midnight by now. So another attempt – same result, although by now, at all the scenes, I think it had at least been moved off the trains so they could be moved out of the stations and the tracks thereby cleared. All except for the Oval, which was still not reacting, so that was removed from the station and taken to the Fort and placed in a magazine cleared for the purpose. I told the others to just stop for the night, we'll come back to it in the morning. Well all right, later that same morning. Go and find somewhere to sleep – if such a thing is possible!

I think I actually did go to bed myself – I may even have slept for an hour or so, and the phone rings. Maybe 04.00 by now? It is the senior investigator at NSY – I'll call him John. "Cliff, why has everything stopped at the scenes? We (i.e. the government) have to have everything running as normal in the morning." "Well, John, everything has stopped because the stuff is reacting; that's very dangerous, and everyone is very tired (including me) and we'll think again in the morning." "Not good enough, what are you going to do?" "It'll have to be good enough, and I don't know." And so on, back and forth. To be fair, he was as sleep deprived as everyone else, and under great pressure from his superiors. And in the past, we at FEL had always been able to give answers and/or advice on what to do, even when different devices or explosives had been used, because they had always been materials we had some knowledge and understanding of. What we had now was something completely new – so different that we hadn't even yet been able to work out exactly *what* it was – a rough idea was all.

Now it seemed like the whole of the UK was waiting for – well, just me, to decide on what should be done next, and how. So was I the only person in the whole of the UK who could decide how to proceed in this part of a significant national threat? How did that happen? Well, in a way it was true. It's a bit like, in a microcosm, a president of a company, or a country – several people could probably do that job, but only one person can actually do it at any one time. And in this particular situation, that person was me. Clearly, I had my own management chain, but no one in that chain would have even the faintest idea of how to proceed, in my opinion at least, and almost certainly not a single one would dream of making a decision on their own. And indeed none had contacted me – for which I was actually grateful. I'm not sure if that was by design – if anything went wrong, they could rightly claim that I was taking decisions on my own that they knew nothing of – or if they actually didn't know how deeply the FEL were involved at that time. Whatever, this sounds appallingly arrogant writing this now, but something had to be done, a plan had to be formed and executed, and there were very few people that I would trust to devise such a plan – all within FEL, and for all of whom I was the immediate line manager. So it was up to me then.

Now, certainly the EXPOs could just have remotely

removed and destroyed the material and its containers, but then we would have no idea what had been used – and the suspects were still out there, maybe with more devices to be set off, which might actually work next time. So that would have been a very poor option which no one wanted, least of all the police.

Anyway, the conversation with John at NSY ended with me saying I would meet with the EXPOs, at their office first thing this morning, and between them, me, and the other FEL staff at the scenes, we would agree a plan and execute it. Best I could do at that moment, so, grudgingly, he accepted that. At the end of all that, I knew there was no point in trying to go back to sleep, so I decided to just get dressed and go into the Fort, before going up to London to meet the EXPOs. I think. I can remember deciding to stay up. I can remember getting a train up to London with Claire, who had dealt with the Oval scene. The steps in between I can't be sure of. Maybe I was sleep walking! I guess I went in to the Fort, and met Claire there – I know she had been there delivering the yellow material from the Oval, in the early hours, so maybe she was still there and I went to see the stuff, then suggested she come with me to the EXPOs. Whatever, we did both go and meet with them.

As we got there we heard the latest news – one of the EXPOs had just got back from clearing the body of Jean Charles de Menezes, who had been shot in Stockwell Tube Station. Since he had been shot in the belief that he likely had some kind of explosive device on him, the EXPOs had been called, as standard procedure, to check and deal with whatever device he might have had. But sadly, as became clear, he had nothing and was nothing to do with any of the bombers. At the time, there was therefore no reason for FEL to be involved in any of that, although much later I was asked to give an opinion on some aspects of that incident. More of that later, suffice it to say here that, in my opinion, if anyone should want to lay any blame on someone for that whole episode, then they should look no further than the dickheads who tried to kill and maim as many people as possible just going about their normal daily lives. As far as I am concerned, he was the single physical casualty of the 21/7 bombers.

Anyway, we all got our heads together, during which I suggested a plan whereby some small (e.g. 200 grams) samples could be taken from the bulk material, to be taken to the Fort for analysis, and we worked out a possible means for transporting the bulk material to a suitable location where it could be destroyed by burning. Once the EXPOs were happy that we had a potentially workable plan (after all, they were the ones that would actually have to implement it!), Claire and I got taken to Warren Street, to check if the situation, at least at one of the scenes, would practically lend itself to the plan we had come up with – which we decided it would. We could only go to one scene (a basic forensic protocol is not to visit multiple scenes in order to avoid possible cross-contamination), and Warren Street was the nearest. So, with the plan in place, Claire and I went back to the Fort. We had included the material from the Oval (which was now at the Fort) in the plan, even though it had so far not reacted like the others – it was still too risky to keep it. We would just sample it, like the rest, with the main bulk being disposed of with the rest. Again, the details of the remainder of the day, up until early evening, escape me, but the FEL was still a blur of activity with the stuff we had so far, while the police were frantically engaged in the biggest manhunt in their history.

It took until early evening, but eventually one of the EXPOs managed to collect up the bulk material from Warren Street Tube and the no. 26 bus in Hackney, and arrived at the Fort to collect the bulk from the Oval Tube, to take it all for disposal at a site he had identified at the fire training area at Biggin Hill Airfield, which was only a short drive from the Fort. He did not have the Shepherd's Bush material, as that had stayed too reactive to transport safely, and it was eventually destroyed somewhere very local, by the EXPO at that scene. I went with the EXPO from the Fort to Biggin Hill, along with a couple of other FEL staff, to see for myself how the material would react when it was burnt (which was the chosen disposal method). It turned out to be quite benign, it just burnt in a controlled manner, but by this time it had probably more or less finished reacting, and it was spread out over quite a big area, unlike previously having been largely clumped together.

So the EXPO went on his way, and we headed back to the Fort, to await the samples from the last scene at Shepherd's Bush, which we had been told were on their way. Soon after we got there I got what I can only describe as an agonised phone call from Andy, the SO15 exhibits officer bringing the samples. "Cliff, the samples are fizzing and bubbling and the van is filling with smoke!"

Now I can't remember exactly what I said, though certainly not what was in my head, which was one stream of expletives! I feel like I must have said just stop and get out and call EXPO, and maybe they did stop briefly, but the end result of the conversation was that they were not far away, and would just go hell for leather to get to us, but just *please, please* be ready to deal with this stuff when we arrive! Which we were, preparing a safe area to put the van in, and every possible bit of kit we could think of, including several large plastic boxes with copious amounts of cold water to put the samples in. I should just say here that water is by no means always the safest way to deal with unknown explosives, but this was based on our very limited understanding of what these particular materials were likely to be. And these were now only samples, not the large bulk amounts we were dealing with earlier. But still, only educated guesswork, and very stressful – for us. I can only imagine the stress levels of Andy and his driver in the van!

Perhaps a bit of perspective would be helpful here. It may seem that, at the one extreme I was being incredibly cavalier here, with stuff that could detonate at any moment, or at the other extreme, was being utterly overdramatic about stuff that really posed very little risk at all. Well, at the time I believed the truth to be somewhere in the middle of that spectrum; based on the admittedly very limited knowledge of the mixture that we had gained at that time, plus some educated guesswork, I thought it was actually quite unlikely that the material would just detonate in its current form. On the other hand, I knew personally of two different incidents in which some not very well understood explosive mixtures had undergone sudden, unexpected, and violent thermal reactions. In one case, someone had suffered life-changing injuries, and in the other case someone died. And these incidents occurred during planned work under controlled conditions on licensed explosives ranges. Well, unpredictable thermal reactions, though not *so far* very violent, were what we were seeing here – with material that we knew was intended to be explosive. So, for me at least, there was a very real level of fear here, but tempered by some educated assumptions, and the urgent need to get enough of the material to test sufficiently to get a proper handle on its composition and properties, in case more devices were ready to be unleashed – the suspects were still at large.

Anyway, I told the MOD police at the Fort gate, that a police vehicle was on its way to us with some vital samples from the London bombings – and they were on NO ACCOUNT to stop this vehicle at the gate (as they normally would) but just wave them straight through. Fortunately they were used to us in FEL and didn't argue. Not sure if there was actually smoke coming from the van at the time – but if there was, that may have convinced them to just stand back and let it through, if they had been in any doubt!

And so the van arrived, the samples still smoking but less so by then (not all of them were smoking, but Andy hadn't stopped to examine them too closely!), and we dealt with them by placing them, still in their containers, in the cold water that we had ready and waiting for them, which (luckily) had the desired effect of cooling them sufficiently to stop them reacting as they had been. As an added precaution, we also divided them up into smaller individual samples, in case they should start up again. And gradually everyone could take some deep breaths and calm down.

Now I can't even begin to describe the list of rules and regulations and general health and safety procedures that we in FEL, at my behest, had ridden absolutely roughshod over and stamped into the dirt, during this whole episode. I can only say that it was an absolutely crazy time, for the FEL, the police, and throughout senior levels of government, and we, along with everyone else, were just doing the best we could to deal with an absolutely unprecedented situation, under enormous pressure. And my own management, either by design or accident, but I'll give them the benefit and say by design, were keeping the lowest of low profiles, which as things worked out, was absolutely the most helpful thing they could do. To be fair, my immediate boss had spoken to me earlier, and said that whatever I needed, I only had to ask, and that he would otherwise just let us all get on with what we needed to do.

23–31 JULY

OK. Maybe time to draw a breath and have a slight change of focus. So far it's mostly been about all the rushing about in the outside world, reacting to one urgent incident after another. Now it's probably worth a look at what's been going on within the lab, which after all is our (FEL staff) normal environment. And in a lab sort of way, it was really just as hectic, but that is rather more difficult to convey than when rushing around in the outside world. Still, I'll give it a go.

With the 7/7 bombings, we had been starting to get a bit of a handle on what we were dealing with, and what our priorities within the lab were. These were basically: What was the explosive main charge? What was the detonator? How were they delivered? How were they triggered? Were they all the same? Anything like them ever seen before? In the UK? Worldwide? If they are completely new devices, where did the technology come from? Is it just one small isolated group, or part of a larger, directed conspiracy? Finding and preserving material suitable for other disciplines, such as fingerprints and DNA.

Of course, with all the material from the Leeds bomb factory, and the Luton Station car, we had a good deal of information to work with, but that still all needed to be positively linked to the actual bombings – because at this point that was still just a working assumption. And this work takes a great deal of time. You have a huge amount of debris, some of which will be very significant, but much of which won't. And since you don't know which is which to start with, you have to actually look at it all, or at least a great deal of it, to get at the really significant stuff. Then you have to examine those bits very closely, and with a variety of tests, to end up with actual concrete evidence, as opposed to simple assumptions, all of which takes a long time. (This is where reality and TV programmes head off in diametrically opposite directions. On TV, people immediately pick up the only and crucial bits of evidence, wave them at a machine or two, and that's job done. If only.)

Now, up until the 21st, particularly after the first ten days or so, the urgency in the lab was slightly tempered by the fact that there were no suspects in custody, and it was starting to look like there weren't going to be, or at least not as main players, only as peripheral offenders, if at all. Then when 21/7 happened, that slight sense of light at the end of the tunnel went right out the window. Now we knew there were going to be prisoners, probably very soon, which meant we needed to get evidence very urgently for the police to be able to charge and remand them. And prisoners there were, I can't remember exactly when, but certainly by 27 July.

Well, the first question now (for both ourselves and the police) was: is this now one investigation or two? Are the 21/7 bombers part of the same group as the 7/7 ones, or are they different? We in the lab still had very little to go on, but we were able to tell the police that the material from the 21/7 devices, although similar, was not the same mixture as that from Leeds (and hence by assumption, the 7/7 bombs). This, combined with the information the police had from their own investigation, led them to decide that they were two separate investigations, which from our point of view made things logistically somewhat easier. The police (well the Met anyway) always give major investigations an operation name. In the past, those names always had some connection, however obscure, to the investigation they related to; a DC of my acquaintance once famously (infamously?) remarked, after an incident in Mincing Street in London, that he would have nothing to do with any investigation called Operation Mincing! Which has nothing to do with anything, but it made me smile at the time. In any event, those days were gone, and names were now produced randomly. And so, 7/7 had been named Operation Theseus, and initially, 21/7 had been kept the same. However, it now became Operation Vivace. Followed, obviously, with lots of debate about how it should be pronounced – choose your own!

Anyway, it made it easier for us in the lab, because we could select out all the Theseus exhibits, and put them on the back burner for the time being, and just concentrate on the Vivace ones – still in the hundreds. There were two main strands to the lab work at this time; one to decide definitively whether these materials could detonate; and one to try and find traces of the detonator explosive.

To have to prove that a main charge in a device is actually an explosive was quite unusual for us. Generally, the materials used are already recognised explosives, and as such, courts will accept that without it needing to be proved again and again. However, when something completely new comes along, it has to be proved to the satisfaction of a court that the material will definitely explode, under the right conditions. And what we were dealing with in both 7/7 and 21/7 was definitely new.

Well, it's not necessarily as simple as it might sound. We did have a test which we could use in the lab, called a cartridge case test. This involves putting about two grams of the test substance into a cartridge (bullet) case, putting a detonator in contact with it, and firing the detonator. The resulting damage to the cartridge case is then compared with the damage caused by a known inert material, such as sand, and a range of other known explosives. This is generally a very good and reliable test, but it does have its limitations, the major one being the size of the sample. Two grams is fine for most commercial explosives, but for many improvised explosives this is at or below the size threshold at which they will properly detonate. Added to which, the samples we had to do the test on had probably changed noticeably from the time they were made and/or used, to when we tested them. All of which meant that we were getting inconsistent and debatable results from this test. And we had got rid of most of the bulk material, because of its unpredictable and very reactive behaviour. So we were struggling with this.

As regards the detonator explosive, perhaps some scene setting might be helpful. High explosives come in two basic forms, primary and secondary. Secondary explosives need a shock wave to make them detonate, generally supplied by a detonator, and are used in large quantities as the main charge. Primary explosives are very sensitive and will detonate readily from various stimuli such as shock, heat, friction, spark, etc. Hence they are used in small quantities, such as in detonators, to provide a shock to detonate a much larger quantity of secondary explosives. It was our working assumption at this point that what had happened with the 21/7 devices was that the detonators had worked properly and exploded, but for unknown reasons they had failed to detonate the main charges. This was based on our own observation of the damage to the devices and the rucksacks they were in, and on witness testimony from people present at the time – there had been a quite loud bang, smoke, torn-open rucksacks on the floor, and in at least one case, the perpetrator had been knocked off his feet.

In the UK, detonators are very tightly controlled and difficult to come by, so if you want to make a bomb using high explosives, in the absence of a commercial detonator, you have to make your own primary explosive. By far the most practical two candidates for this are called HMTD and

TATP (hexamethylene-triperoxide-diamine and triacetone-triperoxide for the technophiles).

Now, here I am going to try and simplify things a bit. Detonators are also sometimes called initiators. And they can come in different sizes, the chosen size being dependent on how sensitive the main charge is. The less sensitive the main charge is, the larger the initiator must be to detonate it. So in the rest of this narrative I will only refer to initiators, not detonators, and I will only refer to the size of initiator as small, medium or large. This is a fairly gross over-simplification, but it is convenient and sufficient for the purposes of the narrative.

Well, we had methods of testing for traces (i.e. amounts invisible to the naked eye) of both HMTD and TATP. However, at that time, we couldn't test for both at the same time – and to change the system from one to the other took at least a day to do, during which time no testing could take place at all. So we had to choose one or the other. Since we now knew that HMTD was present in the Leeds flat, that was the obvious choice, and we had been starting to find some traces of HMTD amongst the 7/7 debris. All blank so far amongst the 21/7 materials, which were now the most important ones, but these were early days – we had a huge number of samples to test, both from the debris, and now also from the suspects, their clothing and their premises.

And then on 23 July a fifth device had been found, abandoned in Little Wormwood Scrubs Park! This was potentially great news, as we now had an intact device to work with – if the EXPO could or would dismantle it manually. This was the subject of a long phone discussion between me and him, as to how he might go about it, if he was prepared to do so at all. As always, a decision entirely up to him, but he did do so and in the process got us a sample of powder from the improvised initiator, and the partially dismantled initiator itself. I really cannot speak too highly of what the EXPOs did (and do); it is often really dangerous work, but then hugely beneficial in terms of the evidence recovered, as against the 'controlled explosion' which is a much safer option but generally provides less really useful evidence. Although the yellow material of the main charge was not reacting at the time, as with the other devices the bulk of it was destroyed locally by the EXPO, but still leaving us maybe 100–200 grams or so for further testing. Which turned out to be crucial.

Meanwhile, in the trace lab, work continued apace looking for traces of HMTD. Separately, the improvised initiator and its powder had been delivered to the lab, and were being dealt with – a necessarily slow and careful process. Even though the amount of powder was only 5–10 grams, this is still sufficient to take fingers off hands, at the very least. So it took a while, but after another two days, this powder had been tested (not by trace techniques – this was a visible quantity so was amenable to other test methods) – and found to be TATP! As it happens, at the moment I had been told this, I had just seen Sarah L coming out of the trace lab – she had been taking a long (maybe two day?) stint in there working up and running samples from her cases. Only one case could be worked on in there at any one time, to avoid any possibility of cross-contamination, so people were taking turns in there. I caught up with her in the lab reception area – and told her the news. I'm sure that is the first time I ever heard her use the F word – several times I think! Being Sarah, it was both shocking and funny in equal measure, though I did try not to laugh, perhaps not entirely successfully. The point was, all that work she had been doing in the trace lab (and others before her on the 21/7 cases) was now just so much wasted time – they had been looking for HMTD. And it's not just a case of putting the same samples down a reset machine – the samples themselves would need re-treatment to make them suitable for the different test.

On the question of whether the main charge material could be made to explode, we had now decided that the cartridge case test was not going to settle this, so we had to look for another approach. Well, there was another test that could be used, called a Large Scale Gap Test (from here onwards simply referred to as a Gap test), which is basically a much bigger version of the cartridge case test. Around 150–200 grams of test material is placed in a steel tube, which is stood upright on a steel plate. A small explosive charge is then placed on the top end of the tube and fired. All the fragments of the steel tube and plate are collected up and photographed, then the process is repeated with an inert material, such as sand, and also with a range of known explosives. Comparing the size of the fragments from the various tests gives a good indication of the explosive power, and type of the test material.

However, although the facilities to do this test were available at the Fort, they were not FEL facilities, so we would need the department that owned those facilities to do this for us. Now, this is not a trivial test, and takes quite a lot of organising and planning to set up, and hence would cause noticeable disruption to that department's own programme of work to just drop everything and do this for us. Not that the individuals who would do the test minded, but their own management certainly would have had an issue with it.

So this was now time for Dstl management to step in and, having said that anything we wanted we only had to ask, I have to say they were as good as their word – no issues were raised, they would get right on it.

Great. Now maybe we could start to make some progress. Except that our samples had other ideas! Up to this point (prior to finding the intact device), although we had got rid of the bulk of the scene materials, we still had a few hundred grams of each, still sitting in the water we had put them in when they had been delivered in a state of some panic, smoking in the van. So, at this point we had enough to do the proposed Gap tests. And then, just about the time we arranged to do these, one of the FEL staff came into the lab, quite breathless, with the news that she had just come from the magazine where the samples were – and the Oval samples, which had so far been the only ones to not show any untoward reactions, had decided to join the party, and were now fizzing and bubbling merrily, even while sitting in their water-filled boxes! And, given all the circumstances up to then, I decided we would have to dispose of most of the rest of the samples, leaving just a few tens of grams in total – plenty for lab tests, but now not enough for the planned Gap tests.

So we finally got a lucky break when the intact device was found, within a day of us thinking we would not have enough for any Gap tests. Now, with that, and combining what we had left from all of the devices (not ideal, but the best we could do), we had enough for one test, and be able to leave enough for any lab tests we still needed to do.

And so, two days later, we had our result – the yellow material from the 21/7 scene would definitely explode, under the right circumstances.

At the end of July, this was the state of play: Three of the four bombers were in custody, along with the one who had abandoned his device. Their premises (at least most of them) had been found and in one in particular, plastic tubs, more of the yellow main charge material, and various other items had been found, firmly linking them to the 21/7 bombs. This was in addition to CCTV footage and fingerprint and DNA evidence on relevant items, so they were charged, on remand, and not going anywhere any time soon. We knew that the 7/7 bombs had been carried in rucksacks, and were made of a ground pepper and hydrogen peroxide main charge, with HMTD initiators. We knew that the 21/7 bombs were made with a flour (or similar material – NOT pepper) and hydrogen peroxide main charge, and had TATP initiators. All of which suggested that the basic design of the devices had come from the same original source, but that the two groups had been working independently from each other.

Also, just around this time, maybe just into August, I remember that the fourth bomber was arrested. He had escaped as far as Italy, but was arrested and held there at the request of SO15. I remember this because FEL was asked to provide some evidence in writing, about his alleged bomb, to support the SO15 request for his extradition to the UK. I can't remember all the details now, but I'm sure Claire, who had the Oval Station case, actually wrote something for them, and I feel like this was yet another late-night request, so maybe I had to countersign what she wrote. At any rate, at some point thereafter, he was duly extradited back to the UK.

AUGUST – NOVEMBER 2005

This is where everything kind of faded from the public view, but for FEL it was where the hard grind of the mountain of lab work that had built up really began. By the end of this period, over 2,000 separate pieces of evidence had been submitted for examination, just in relation to the 7/7 and 21/7 bombings, but of course there was still the day-to-day work which came in on a regular basis, which also had to be dealt with. We had one bit of luck here – we had fairly recently lost one of our senior staff, who had gone to work for a forensic lab in Scotland. I got in touch with him, just on the off chance that he might come back for a while – I was thinking maybe we could come to some arrangement with his lab to 'borrow' him for a while. But it turned out that he was actually quite interested in returning full-time. Normally this would involve all sorts of bureaucratic hoops to go through, and take months, even if his lab was fully cooperative. Well, I think they must have been, but also our own management must have gone into overdrive, because as it turned out, he was back working in the lab by early August – which must have been the quickest re-employment of anyone in Dstl ever! Added to this, another of our staff, who had been away on secondment to another organisation, was snatched back and again, working in the lab by early August.

These two extra staff were a real boon to us, and everyone had been working lots of overtime, but it still wasn't enough. The biggest bottleneck now was work going through our trace lab, which only had a limited number of relevant machines, and which, as noted somewhere above, was very limited in how many items could be worked on at any one time. And we were having to work to a court deadline of early November for committal proceedings – this is the initial procedure in setting up a full trial, where each side outlines its case, pleas are made by the defendants, and dates are set. This meant that at least interim statements would be required from the relevant FEL staff on their findings from all the (21/7) cases, by then.

And so we did something that, to my knowledge, had never been done in the history of FEL – we started a two-shift working pattern, from 7 am–11 pm I think. This may not seem like a very big deal to some people, but the civil service very rarely works this way, and FEL is a civil service lab. It is a full forensic lab, there are always at least two people on-call 24/7, and it can and occasionally does, work at any time of the day or night or weekends. But this is just if necessary to deal with a particular incident, and FEL had never previously had anything approaching this scale to deal with.

If you are wondering about exactly how much history FEL has, well, its first incarnation was in the 1880s – it still has some of the bound ledgers from around that time! This was in response to a series of so called 'Fenian Outrages' – wouldn't you know it, basically Irish terrorism! Cycles of history, huh? OK, at the time, it was only an investigator (Colonel Majendie) and a chemist (Dr Dupree), and probably an assistant or two, but that was the start of the FEL, and it has continued in one form or another up to the present day. So it has some pedigree.

I can't remember how long this went on for, a few weeks I think, but it was certainly a landmark for the FEL, and I put this in here, just to try and convey the sense of continuing pressure at the lab, not just in the first three to four weeks, but in the months following on from that.

DECEMBER – NEW YEAR 2006

I am going to digress briefly here – a bit more personal stuff, not really about the 7/7 and 21/7 story, except how it relates to me as a personal recollection. So if you just want the story bit, skip to the next heading, and you won't miss anything. This is really just for my benefit. Call it another, rather long-winded, musing on the possible merits of some sort of counselling after such kinds of incidents.

Back in 2004, Vanessa and I had started to think a little bit about what we might do when I retired. I said I had occasionally wondered about having a boat – something with a cabin and an engine; hadn't thought further than that. Well, she was really enthusiastic about the idea, so we thought – let's buy a boat now, I could do some courses, we could use it in the summertime, and get used to it, so that when I did retire we'd both be ready to do some real trips, maybe around the British coast, over to France, really spend some time with it, and each other. So we did buy a boat, 30 foot, proper big cabin, cooking facilities, comfortable double bed in the main cabin, and two small extra berths in a small aft cabin, nice aft deck. We bought it in Southampton and sailed it round to Brighton, where it was to be berthed. I think this was early August. Then within two or three weeks – Vanessa was diagnosed with breast cancer. Well, that basically wiped out the rest of the summer, with all her tests and then treatment, taking us right into 2005, without hardly using the boat at all. Now by about June 2005, her treatment was mostly over, certainly the intensive stuff, so we both thought – OK, this summer we'll really get back into the boating thing. And then 7/7 happened. So, as must be apparent from all the foregoing, I was effectively gone for the whole of the summer again, and the boat just sat there for another year.

So when it came to December again, I suppose I sort of took stock. I don't know how many hours of overtime I had worked by then, but many hundreds. Normally I wouldn't get paid for overtime, at that level some is informally expected, and anything more than a few hours is then supposed to be taken as time off at a convenient time. Well, that clearly couldn't happen – I'd be off for months! An exception was made for this particular situation, and I was given a payment for some of the overtime – which meant that I had some unexpected extra cash. So I suggested to Vanessa that we go away somewhere for Christmas and New Year – and we would fly business class! – something she'd never done, and was really excited about. We settled on the Florida Keys. And we did have a wonderful holiday.

But what's the point of all this? As I recall it, I was just thinking, we've missed out on a summer holiday, it's been a difficult time, let the world go hang for a couple of weeks and have a decent break. The subtext being that everything will be fine again after the break. I never had a conscious thought that maybe I had changed a bit, but now I think maybe I had – and maybe that had affected Vanessa too. Or maybe subconsciously I was aware of something. At any rate, after this year, the joy had gone out of the boat, certainly for me, and maybe for Vanessa, or maybe she just saw that in me. I eventually sold it in 2009. This is the same mental territory I wandered into earlier, which I then left alone, and which I thought I could come back to in digressing here. Except that again, suddenly, I get a real sense of treading on thin ice – so maybe it is best to just leave it alone. OK, perhaps there is something to be dug out here, but what purpose would it serve now? I'm functioning OK (I think anyway), and thanks to the cancer Vanessa's no longer here, so there's no relationship to rescue or work on. Perhaps it would have helped at the time, but it's too late to change anything now, so why dwell on it?

In summary, I'm more inclined to think now, than I was then, that some sort of counselling, at the time of a major incident, is probably a good idea. Enough.

PAGAN TRUFFLE

What!? Well, quite. Dstl has its own random naming system when it wants to give a name to some particular project – and this is the kind of result you get!

By Christmas, the judicial process for 21/7 was well under way, and I had been advised by prosecution counsel that the main argument by the defence, in the upcoming trial, was likely to be that the devices weren't intended to explode and harm people, nor could they – they were just intended to scare people. There was no dispute that they had actually made and operated the devices. This being the case, counsel asked me if, and how, we could show that not to be the case, i.e. to prove that the devices, as constructed, could explode.

Well, this would require a significant programme of explosive trials, and since we knew very little about the properties of these types of mixtures, that would be quite a major project. This is not something the FEL could do itself, but there was another Dstl department, also based at the Fort, that did precisely this kind of work. After discussions with them – I will call them Explosives Group (EG) for convenience – I advised counsel that this work could be done, but it would take a minimum of six months, and it would mean the EG suspending their current work programme to do it. And that would need instruction from a very high level, beyond just Dstl, to make it happen. So, at the committal proceedings in December, prosecution counsel made this application to the judge, and after a lot of robust discussion from all concerned, the judge eventually ruled that this work was in the national public interest, and needed more urgently than their current work programme, and thus made a court order that it be done – to be completed for the start of the trial, by early June 2006. This was quite an interesting reminder to me of just how much power senior judges have – not much stands in the way of a court order.

And so project Pagan Truffle was born. From my point of view, this was a good outcome – but there was a downside. This work would ultimately have to be written as a legal statement and presented in court, and cross-examined as the defence saw fit. The EG could do all the work, but they are not forensic scientists, and they were very clear that they would write a scientific report, as normal, but had no intention of presenting this in court – which I actually agreed with. In principle, scientific work should not be presented in criminal trials by non-forensic scientists, unless completely unavoidable – and in a part of this case that did happen, actually on both sides. And although not fully apparent at the time, in both instances where non-forensic scientists did give evidence, it did not go well for them, some consequences of which are still being felt to this day! More of that later. Anyway, to get round this issue for Pagan Truffle, the EG would basically be deemed to be working under my direct supervision, by which means, I would be the one to actually write a legal statement and present it as evidence in court. This is a standard way of working in forensic labs: court-going forensic scientists (case officers) clearly can't physically do every test or examination themselves; they use assistants, who generally do not have to give evidence – they are deemed to be directed and supervised by the relevant case officer. But the supervision must be real, which meant I would have to spend a lot of time with the EG, with their planning, and preparation – and most importantly when they did the explosive firings. Fun for some of the time (childish, but who doesn't like blowing stuff up?), but yet more time away from home, since this couldn't be done at the Fort – these explosive firings were too big to be carried out there. And more stress for me, I was somewhat out of my comfort zone here, some of these EG scientists really are rocket scientists!

The question was – under what conditions could these mixtures explode, if at all? All we really knew at this point was that they consisted of flour and hydrogen peroxide. We only had a limited time and could only do a limited number of tests, so what to choose? The size of charge chosen was nominally five kilograms, based on the size of the container of the abandoned device. Eventually we came up with a list of twenty-four variations of this five-kilogram charge to test, which was the practical maximum we thought we could do in the time available. First we had to choose what ratios of flour and hydrogen peroxide. From a theoretical chemistry perspective, it is possible to work out, approximately, what the most efficient ratio is likely to be, so we chose that, and then one ratio either side of that, giving us three different ratios. But hydrogen peroxide is available in different strengths, so each of those ratios would be made up with one of two different strengths of hydrogen peroxide. One was a strength that could be easily bought by the general public, the other was the strongest commercially available, which cannot be bought by the general public, only by accredited commercial users. So this now gave six variations. But we also wanted to know if, and how quickly, such mixtures would be likely to deteriorate with time – very likely, given their highly reactive nature. So each of the above mixtures was made and then left for one day and five days before firing, it being felt likely they would be made on one day then used the next (the mixing is not a quick process), or at least not left for longer than five days before being used. Now we have twelve variations. Finally, each of those twelve variations would be fired with two sizes of initiator – a medium size one, and one several times bigger, this (large) size being chosen as the size at which, if the mixtures don't explode, then they are probably not going to explode under any conditions. Which gave us our twenty-four test firings.

By the end of May the results were in. And they told us that with the weaker hydrogen peroxide, none of the mixtures would explode. However, with the stronger hydrogen peroxide, all the mixtures showed some reaction, with the chemically most efficient flour/hydrogen peroxide ratio mixtures, all detonating fully and reliably under all the other conditions. So flour and hydrogen peroxide mixtures can indeed make effective and reliable explosives – but only within a certain range of mixtures. At the end of our planned tests, we had a spare day, and some spare mixtures left, so we did two more firings. Despite the results we had got, I still felt that the size and make-up of the bombers' initiators would be an issue – they had used TATP, an improvised explosive, not possible on safety grounds for us to replicate on these tests. So on the last day we made two duplicate devices with the most efficient mixtures, and fired them, each using just a small size initiator – much smaller than the medium size initiator we had been using to test the mixtures up to then. And both detonated. To the eye, these were still full detonations, but on the instrumentation, we could see that in one case, the detonation was not quite a full one – an important observation which suggested that the shock from a small commercial initiator was perhaps right on the edge of what is required to make such mixtures explode. And this was probably as close as we could safely get at that time to the shock the bombers' own initiators would have actually produced.

THE FORENSIC EVIDENCE –
PRE-TRIAL (FOR 21/7)

Before I get properly into the legal side of this story, I need to be clear on where I am coming from in writing this. This is a personal recollection of a significant episode in my life, written from an absolutely personal perspective. As such, it may be that it gives the impression, at times, that the evidence I, and other staff at the FEL, gave at the trial was the main contributor to the final outcome. Such an impression would be wrong. In any trial, the final outcome is the result of the court's consideration of all of the evidence presented to it, and in this case in particular, there was a huge amount of evidence given by a large number of people and organisations. No single part of that evidence should be deemed more important than any other, it is the sum total of all the evidence that counts. My evidence was no more or less important than that of the other FEL staff, or anyone else involved in the case. So it is in no sense an objective chronicle of how the trial progressed, nor is it a commentary on how the court came to its conclusions. It is simply my recollection of my own involvement in a significant national event, seen from a distance of over ten years.

Now, while Pagan Truffle had been going on, back in the lab we had not been idle. Amongst the large amount of material that had been examined were various pieces of equipment and other items taken from the premises believed to be the main 21/7 bomb factory in London. The equipment included a number of aluminium pans, that all showed signs of severe corrosion, and amongst the other items were several empty bottles of hydrogen peroxide hair products. The corrosion damage was shown to have been likely caused by exposure to hydrogen peroxide (I think this was determined by the Forensic Science Service Lab in London, not FEL). This only really made sense if they had been used to heat the hydrogen peroxide – which in turn only really made sense if they were being used to make the hydrogen peroxide from the bottles, into a more concentrated form. Precisely what would be required to make an effective explosive with flour.

And this brings us to a key question, which we had not been able to answer explicitly – and neither had any other laboratory. How concentrated was the hydrogen peroxide in the actual mixtures recovered? As noted above, we had to get rid of most of it; all we had left were small samples. And neither we, nor anyone else had a proven method for doing this analysis – unsurprisingly perhaps, since there had never been a need for that before!

Now, it is the nature of forensic science, that all measurements, and tests should only be done using procedures that have been demonstrated, to the satisfaction of the profession, to produce reliable results, i.e. they have been properly validated. Which is a lengthy process. So, while there were ways we could have tried to measure the concentration of hydrogen peroxide in the mixtures, we could not have produced a reliable method in time for court. Or, even more to the point, within the time that the original samples could still realistically be considered close to how they had started out – i.e. before they had 'gone off' (in the milk sense).

To try and get round this, I had arranged for another series of Gap tests to be done, using a range of different mixtures and strengths of hydrogen peroxide and flour. Comparing the results of those Gap tests with the single one we had done with the actual material recovered from the scenes, would give us at least an approximation of which of these known mixtures was closest to the actual material. These Gap tests showed that the scene material was closest to a mixture where the strength of the hydrogen peroxide was sufficient for the mixture to reliably explode, but not reliably from a small initiator – it would need at least a medium size to make it reliable.

To my mind, we now had reliable evidence, to a good approximation, of the composition of the scene material and, in particular, to the fact that it could reliably explode under the right circumstances. And just as importantly, the Gap tests are easily understood – they are based on a simple assessment of the metal fragments produced, and a visual estimation of fragment size, which the jury could see for themselves – they were photographed for this purpose.

Unfortunately, this very simplicity was a bit of a disappointment to the police – they will always take 'super science' over a basic visual test, if it is available. And at the FEL over the past couple of years, we had been researching a new analytical technique called Isotope Ratio Mass Spectrometry (IRMS) – which is indeed 'super science'. However, we were looking at this for just some very specific types of analysis, and even with those, it was still a research tool, absolutely not for court use at that time. But for some reason, which I didn't understand then, and still don't now, the police got the idea that this could be used to tell us the strength of the hydrogen peroxide in the scene material – and in a much more 'scientific' way. So they asked me if the FEL could do this analysis for them – which I flatly refused. I explained that we were still learning about the technique, and even then only for specific uses that most certainly did not include what they were asking for. So, when they finally realised it simply wasn't going to happen at the FEL, they asked me if we could recommend someone who could do it for them. To which I said, "No, we can't, it's highly unlikely anyone with a forensic background could or would do this, it's the wrong technique, you don't need it, and if you *do* find someone, there will just be a big argument between experts in court, which *no one* will understand. All it will do is muddy the water, which is currently not muddy!" If this gives you the impression that I was irritated because they wouldn't just let it go, you would be correct!

Anyway – they wouldn't let it go. And failing to find any forensic lab that could or would do it, they found an academic, at a university. Now this person was using IRMS for another, different type of analysis to what we were doing – and also, nothing like what was being asked in this case. And while he was no doubt an expert with the technique in his own field, like everyone else, he would be starting from scratch with the question being posed (i.e. how strong was the hydrogen peroxide in the mixture?). Neither was he a forensic scientist and, in my opinion, he had no idea what he was getting into. I will come back to this later, but basically the seeds were sown here for a potential appeal after the trial had finished.

Meanwhile, preparations for trial continued, not just at the FEL, but by all parties involved, and the start of the trial duly arrived in October 2006. And only then (having seen the prosecution case) did the defence advance their case that: – yes such mixtures could explode – but not with their TATP initiators; their flour/hydrogen peroxide ratio was different to the three ratios we tested; and yes they did concentrate their hydrogen peroxide, but then they diluted their mixtures after having done this! Which to me made no sense whatsoever – why go to all that trouble (it's several days' work to concentrate the required quantity of hydrogen peroxide), just to dilute it again? But hey, what do I know? So now these questions had to be specifically addressed. Could a TATP initiator cause a flour and hydrogen peroxide mixture to explode, and, if so, under what conditions? Well the judge was (understandably) seriously pissed off by this turn of events, because it led to a whole series of discussions as to if, and how, we could now answer these new questions, and it would clearly require a significant adjournment.

Enter Qinetiq (pronounced kinetic... so why not just... oh, never mind). Qinetiq is a private company, also based at the Fort, which was originally a part of the MOD, but had been sold off to private industry. Although the EG had a lot of facilities, they did not, at the time, have the ability to make and fire significant quantities of TATP. Which Qinetiq did but, as with most parts of this saga, there were some complications. One was that the TATP had to be used on site; it could not be transported off site for safety reasons. This in turn meant that any test explosions with the flour/hydrogen peroxide mixtures, using TATP initiators, would have to be done on site. This would limit the size of the devices we could make to around 500 grams; the Fort was not a big enough site to be able to fire larger amounts than this. And then a rig would have to be devised that could hold the main charge, and separately hold the TATP initiator, and then bring them together remotely, immediately before firing. Quite rightly, safety considerations absolutely ruled out the possibility of manually adding an improvised TATP initiator to an improvised explosive charge – to do that would carry a real risk of killing someone.

Eventually, after long discussions with Qinetiq, and then the judge, a plan was agreed. At times the discussions were quite surreal – e.g. "How many hours does it take to make a remote firing rig?" The judge asked me this when I was explaining how long and complicated this new set of tests was going to be, probably three months, and giving these rigs as an example. They would have to be designed, tested and built, and several of them, since for every test that exploded, the rig would be destroyed, and a new one needed for the next test. Clearly, I thought, one lengthy part of a lengthy process then. So when he asked me this question, I was rather lost for words! I was thinking, "Why not ask me how long is a piece of string?!" Probably not the best response to a senior judge! I think I said something like, "Errm, well, I have no idea, my Lord – these are not off the shelf items, I was just trying to illustrate why the whole testing programme will take a long time." He, of course, was just generally grumpy about the new delay, and how long it was going to be.

It was eventually agreed that it would take until early New Year 2007. We would do a variety of 500 gram explosive charges (including exactly what they said they had made), that could be remotely loaded with TATP initiators, and fired at the Fort. So finally, grudgingly, the trial was moved to start, I think, in January of 2007.

As an aside, and just as an indication of how much work is involved in all these explosive tests, half a million pounds would not be a bad estimate of how much they cost in total – all at the taxpayers' expense. If all of the defence case had been known at the start of the judicial process, this would have been much less, maybe even half. Not just because of this, but because of the delays in general, the judge was quite scathing after the trial about these tactics by the defendants and their advisers.

Anyway, the tests were all carried out, and the results showed that TATP initiators, of the size accepted by the defendants, could reliably detonate flour and hydrogen peroxide mixtures if the hydrogen peroxide was concentrated enough. The mixture they said they had made could also explode, but not reliably and only with a medium size initiator, not with the shock from one of their TATP initiators.

However, the various Gap tests showed (to my mind anyway) that the scene material was not the same as what they now claimed they had made (a Gap test was done on that mixture too, for comparison). The Gap tests showed that the scene material was more easily exploded than the mixture claimed by the defendants, most closely matching a mixture with the most efficient flour/hydrogen peroxide ratio, but with its hydrogen peroxide slightly less concentrated. Its actual concentration was sufficient to enable it to perform as a reliable explosive, but only with a medium size initiator, larger than had been used in the devices. Close but not quite close enough. But this line is not an exact one, and nor could it ever be – such mixtures are never completely homogenous, which will affect how they react. Think of mixing custard, or mashed potato – anyone ever had lumps in that!? And the process of concentrating hydrogen peroxide by heating it up is a very inexact one, especially in a kitchen type environment – without proper equipment only a broad estimate of the strength you have achieved is possible. And if you go too far with it, you are likely only to degrade what you have already produced.

Basically, in my opinion, the defendants did everything they needed to, to make viable explosive devices – they just didn't quite get their hydrogen peroxide concentrated enough to work on the day.

So what, you may ask, about the IRMS? Wasn't that supposed to give a definite (and 'properly scientific') answer to the question of how concentrated the hydrogen peroxide in the scene mixture was? Well, yes it was. And the person who did that test got an answer of almost exactly what the Gap tests gave me, but in number form rather than just an approximate visual interpretation. So that's job done then? Oh, if only! This IRMS discussion sits more naturally, later in this narrative. For now I will say only this: I did not have, and do not have an opinion on the IRMS work, whether it is right or wrong, done well or badly. I am not expert enough (and neither are most other people). But more than that, as far as I am concerned, it is an irrelevance. My opinions, as expressed above, and in court, rest on all the explosive tests, Gap tests, and the many other analyses that were done. For completeness, I will add here that, since the trial, FEL have developed a method for doing this analysis, for use if necessary in the future – using a well understood, reliable chemical test, that has nothing to do with IRMS. It just wasn't available at the time.

THE TRIAL

Finally, about eighteen months after the incidents, the trial for the 21/7 bombings got under way. (7/7 was still in the background, but taking a back seat, as there were no main defendants alive for trial in that case.) For 21/7, there were six defendants. Four had set off their devices, in which the initiators had functioned, but had failed to set off the main charge. One had abandoned his device in Little Wormwood Scrubs. I can't remember how the sixth person was involved, but I seem to recall he was not actually in the country at the time, so maybe as an instigator, or helper.

There were a number of possible charges, some relating to the making of explosives (such as the TATP), and using explosives in public, and no doubt others. These would have been very easy to prosecute, and would result in a number of years in jail – but nowhere near life. So the prosecution chose the big one – conspiracy to murder, which would certainly allow for very long (effectively life) sentences. And as I recall it, they chose to prosecute *only* this charge – a high-risk strategy indeed, especially considering no one had died at any of the scenes! The reasoning was, that if you give the jury some easy options to find them guilty, they may be less inclined to find them guilty for a more complicated and difficult charge. Understandable, but definitely a brave decision – sometimes senior prosecutors really do earn their big bucks!

And so the trial got under way. Over several days, the FEL staff gave their evidence about each individual case, and then I gave my evidence about all of the explosive tests, and then an overall view of the FEL evidence, and how it all linked together. Basically, as described above, the devices contained a viable initiator explosive (which worked); a viable main charge of explosive (that failed to detonate); the reason they failed was that the hydrogen peroxide was slightly less concentrated than it needed to be; and it was not possible under all of the circumstances of manufacture of these devices, for *anyone* to justifiably predict that they would not work. Basically, in my opinion, these devices were intended to kill as many people as possible just going about their daily business – as had happened on 7/7. They just (thankfully) got their mixtures slightly wrong.

We were all cross-examined, as you would expect, but I don't remember any of it being particularly difficult or aggressive. The one bit that does stick in my mind, was about my decision to dispose of the bulk of the material from the scenes. This was presented as me 'playing the safety card' – implying, I felt, that I had chosen to do this, with at least the thought that it would then be difficult to properly test the scene material, in case such proper testing would be of more benefit to the defence. Normally I would just take this as part of the expected 'game playing' that is very common in criminal trials – ours is an adversarial system, and no matter what anyone tells you, it is not an earnest search by all for the truth. Each side wants to win and they will do whatever they can, within the rules, to achieve that. But on this occasion, and for the only time I can remember, I was really annoyed by this implication. 7/7 had just happened and many people had died; all we knew was that this 21/7 material appeared to be something similar, and it was reacting vigorously and unpredictably. Added to which, as mentioned above, I personally knew of two occasions where different, but poorly understood, mixtures had reacted similarly, killing one person and seriously injuring another. And now some armchair critic (the defence expert – I shall come to this shortly), with no practical knowledge and what seemed to me a very poor understanding of explosives was implying, via his counsel, that I was being deliberately overcautious.

Well I can't say how my answer came across, but I said words to the effect that I had personal knowledge of how dangerous it could have been; no one who worked for me was going to be put in harm's way if I could help it; I was not prepared to speculate or theorise about these mixtures at that time, because that could kill someone; and I really couldn't care less what someone who lacked the knowledge to do anything other than speculate and theorise, thought about this! Hopefully some irritation showed through, because I was seriously irritated. And certainly nothing came back at me.

So that was the FEL evidence. But there was still the IRMS evidence to come and then the defence expert's evidence. Well, I had given my evidence about Gap tests and all the rest, and my opinion on the mixtures, but still it was the IRMS that everyone was interested in and impressed with as far as the concentration of the hydrogen peroxide was concerned. I should say, at this point, that the guy who carried out the IRMS analysis, also did various other analyses of the scene residues which were really useful, and added significant support to what I had said about this question. These analyses were by standard, recognised and accepted methods of analysis, and I had no problem with them. The IRMS analysis however, was none of these things.

Anyway, the IRMS evidence was presented, along with all the other analyses that had been done alongside it. Well, the other work was cross-examined, but it all seemed a bit cursory. The IRMS was really where it was all at. It must have taken at least a day to present, maybe longer. And probably no one in court understood it properly, including me. The judge probably did as well as anybody there – I think he is one of those super bright people that can just pick out the salient points of whatever he is presented with, no matter how complicated, but even he was clearly having to work very hard to make proper sense of it. So when it came to cross-examination, the defence really struggled to make much headway – not helped by the fact that their own expert also had absolutely no expertise in IRMS.

Well, what's the problem you might well ask? The IRMS findings actually back up what I have said, and the person who did it has no connection with the FEL, it's not FEL's evidence, so even if it goes wrong, it's not our problem. Largely correct. But not entirely. I will come back to this.

THE DEFENCE EXPERT

It is normal, where expert witness evidence is a significant part of a case, for the defence to appoint their own expert – and it is important for them to do this, expert testimony should be properly tested. This doesn't always mean that there must be an argument in court; often much scientific evidence can be agreed between experts, prior to the trial. Indeed the judge tried very hard to get this to happen in this case, and as a result I had a number of meetings with the defence expert, but in the end, agreement over anything other than the most basic aspects proved impossible.

Why? I think there were two main stumbling blocks. First, he was an academic, with absolutely no knowledge of the forensic process. The IRMS guy was also not a forensic scientist, but I believe he at least had an awareness of some of the concepts of forensic science. But the defence expert seemed unaware that forensic science even had any concepts. The second stumbling block was that he started from a position, at least as it seemed to me, that as a professor and senior academic, his job was to help out these well-meaning but slightly second-tier government scientists, with all and any science in this case. Second-tier because otherwise they'd be top research scientists such as himself, obviously.

In his defence, my recollection is that defending counsel had tried hard to get an established forensic, or explosives scientist to act for them, and had been turned down by every such person they had approached. So they had had to widen their circle, to include people who had neither a forensic, nor an explosives background, and to be fair, initially he had also been reluctant to get involved, but eventually he was persuaded. There was no malice or bad faith in him, but as a senior scientist he should have recognised that he was the one in a new environment, and that he needed to learn and adapt to it. But in my opinion he failed to grasp that, and simply behaved as what he probably was – the kindly professor who did the teaching, while those around him did the learning. Unless they were his peers, which we weren't because we weren't senior academics.

So, as part of his lack of understanding of the forensic scientist's role, he seemed to think that he had to disagree with every aspect of the prosecution scientific evidence. Whereas what he should have been doing was examining every bit on its scientific merits. Which he was also poorly equipped to do, since he was largely outside his own field of expertise. So in the end, we were unable to come to any sensible agreement about any significant part of my evidence.

Interestingly, he seemed to find it much easier to agree with some of the IRMS guy's evidence, presumably because he was a fellow senior academic and therefore a peer, and thought the IRMS work was largely quite impressive. This was despite the fact that he had no expertise in IRMS whatsoever, as even the judge noted at one point!

Anyway, the prosecution had finished its scientific evidence, now it was the turn of the defence. And it did not go well for their expert. He did not provide his reports when he was supposed to, he did not have proper notes to back up the experiments he had done, he had used the wrong methods, those that he had used were not validated to demonstrate that they actually worked, a concept he seemed unaware of, or at least entirely uninterested in. And when it came to his cross-examination, he really suffered. Now, I can't help but feel some sympathy for him; it is frequently an uncomfortable place to be, and given how unprepared he was for it, it must have been a very bad experience for him. Indeed, I believe I was told afterwards by someone, that he had said he would never touch anything to do with court ever again, and wouldn't have done so in the first place if he had had any idea of what was in store for him.

Having said that, my sympathy was severely limited by the fact that he apparently made little or no effort to look up at least some basic parameters of the various sciences he was talking about. At one point in his evidence he had talked about 'ideal explosives' but the way he had used this term made me wonder if he actually knew what that meant, or if he thought it was just a general term for 'best'. So when I was asked about his evidence by the prosecution counsel, I mentioned this, saying I couldn't quite believe he would not know (or have checked up) that this had a specific meaning, but if he wanted some questions to ask, that might be one. Which he did – and so the professor squirmed as it transpired that no, he didn't know it had a specific meaning, nor what that might be. And this was just one small part of his cross-examination. Very uncomfortable I'm sure, especially for someone unused to being challenged on his own knowledge, by people he did not consider peers – but then he should have at least bothered to do some reading up beforehand. So, like I said, I had some sympathy, but not a great deal.

MILLIE

Another brief digression here, nothing to do with the trial, just another memory from the time that has just popped into my head – but I just feel like giving my cat, Millie, a mention! Around this time I was going into court on most days, not to give evidence, I was finished with that, but to be there to advise the prosecution counsel, if he needed it, while he was cross-examining the defence expert. Well I think it may have been a half-term holiday, because my wife (who was a teacher) was away visiting her sister, who was also a teacher. As I was getting ready to go one morning, I noticed our cat in the back garden, lying on the lawn. She was an elderly cat by then but was still getting along OK – but she hadn't come in for her food, and lying on the lawn was not something she would normally do. So I went out to have a look, see if she would come in for some food. Well she got up as I reached her, but showed no interest in coming in so I left her there to carry on sorting myself out – and noticed she had just laid down again. This was definitely not right, so I went back out, picked her up and carried her in to her basket, where she just lay down again. A quandary now – I should take her to the vet, but I had to go to the court, and there was no one else around to take her. So I thought, I will go to court, tell them my cat is poorly, and see if I can get away early and then take her to the vet. Well, they were all very sympathetic, if I could just stay for a couple of hours that would probably be OK, and I could go then. So I did that, got home about midday – and she was still lying in the same position I had left her in – not a good sign.

Worse when I touched her, she was cold – and stiff! Well this was a bit of a shock – I really hadn't realised how bad she was – and a very sad moment; I certainly did shed a few tears. But she had had a good life, and I think she must have died very soon after I put her in her basket, so I don't think she suffered much, if at all. But what now? I thought about putting her in the garden, but it was only a small one and I would have struggled to dig a hole big enough in the space available. OK then – maybe the vet would take her? Is that something people do with dead pets? So I phoned them and said my cat had died, could they deal with it? Then followed a somewhat surreal saga – sad for sure, but (as it seemed to me) also a bit funny in a dark sort of way. A moment of silence on the phone, then, "Oh this must be a mistake, none of our cats here has died." Silence from me while I worked that out. Then I said, "No, my cat is not with you, she is here with me, and she's dead." Another moment, then, "Oh, sorry, I see – are you sure she's dead?" "Errm, well she's cold, completely unresponsive – and very stiff!" "Oh I see, well yes, of course, bring her in and we'll have a look." I wasn't sure about the need for the 'have a look', but I let that go. So, I got her vet box out to put her in – but now she wouldn't fit, because of the rigor mortis! I struggled for a bit, but finally had to put her in upside down – with her legs all poking out of the top of the basket! And in that undignified pose I got her to the vet and carried her into the reception – attracting some strange looks from other people there, while I waited for someone ahead of me to be dealt with. And after a few moments I was dealt with – very quickly, when the receptionist worked out what it was that was attracting attention from other people in reception! So goodbye Millie, and rather sadly home to phone Vanessa. Who was also naturally upset, but then quite relieved that she hadn't been there to have had to deal with it by herself, which she otherwise would have been. And just to round this little saga off, when I got back to the court the next day, at one point someone remembered about me going off early to take my cat to the vet, and asked, as you do, how my cat was. Which caused a moment's slightly stunned silence when I replied something like – "Oh... err... well, not good really. Well, actually she was dead!" But then I related the story, which sort of broke the tension, and then we all got back to the business of the ongoing trial.

I'm not sure why this little vignette should stick so clearly in my mind – but I look back on it, strangely, as a rather fond memory. Perhaps because it was a significant enough piece of everyday life, even if a little sad, to tear my mind away from the all-consuming concentration on all things 21/7, and to remind me, if only briefly, that real life could matter more than work.

THE TRIAL – CONTINUED...

The trial went on for several months in total, of which the scientific evidence was maybe only two or three weeks, which I say only to make the point again that there was a great deal of evidence, of which the science was only one part, but this is a personal account from memory, not a trial log, and these are just the bits that I remember which involved me. But I had invested a great deal of time and effort in getting to this point, so I (along with all others involved) naturally had a great deal of interest in the outcome.

The outcome was that the four main bombers were convicted and sentenced to life terms, with a minimum of forty years before they would be eligible for parole. Which to my mind was a good outcome, since it meant that the FEL's and my evidence (amongst others), to the effect that the devices were designed and intended to kill, had been accepted by the jury. The other two defendants the jury could not agree on, but they were always going to be more contentious, since one had abandoned his device, and the other wasn't actually there at the time. But since the jury could not agree, as opposed to them being acquitted, a retrial for them was ordered.

The retrial was scheduled for later that year, but in the event it wasn't actually held because both defendants pleaded guilty shortly before it was due to start. This was a good thing, meaning no one had to go and give evidence again, but in any case, the build-up had been much less frenetic than for the original trial, since most of the evidence was exactly the same. The only extra work I can remember for the retrial (for me anyway), was that I had to examine a sideboard taken from the main bomb-making premises, which the defendant who had abandoned his device claimed had been booby-trapped, but which he had disarmed after the others had gone. At the end of my examination, I concluded that there was some evidence to suggest that this might have happened, but I couldn't be sure. Whether this had any effect I have no idea, but the final outcome was that, having pleaded guilty, they both received several years' sentences, however, much less than the four main bombers. Which seemed like a pretty uncontroversial result to me.

So that's the end of the saga then? No, of course not. It seems like it's in the nature of major trials to almost inevitably be appealed at some point – and this case was no exception, which I will come to shortly. But first, for the sake of keeping it chronological, I will round this part off by returning to what started it all – 7/7.

Although that took a back seat while 21/7 was dealt with, there was still a legal process to go through and, for the FEL staff, all the evidence collected from those incidents still had to be examined, written up and reported, though clearly not under the same pressure as for 21/7. Eventually there was a trial, but this was of a number of alleged helpers, since the main perpetrators were dead. My only involvement with this trial was to provide evidence of how the devices were constructed, and to offer my opinion that it was very unlikely that the four bombers could have designed and produced their devices completely in isolation – they would have had to at least been given some advice and information to have produced such effective devices from scratch. All of which was pretty uncontroversial, since it didn't relate directly to these specific defendants, merely that *someone* must have helped. Anyway, this trial ended with the jury unable to agree about any of the defendants – so a retrial was ordered! And at the end of that, I think two were found guilty of having attended terrorist training camps in the Middle East, and the rest were acquitted.

And finally there was an inquest for the 7/7 incidents. For which I gave pretty much the same evidence as for the trial. In this case it was perhaps slightly more significant because I was also asked to address some conspiracy theories (of which many abounded), and specifically one which held that the bombs were placed underneath the trains, and hence not by the identified bombers but by – state agents? – other shadowy organisations? – space aliens? – who knows?... Well they weren't. Placed underneath the trains that is. And I could give very definite evidence on that.

And so, by sometime in 2008, the saga was over. Or so I thought. And it was for a while, but then came the application to appeal which, while not directly relating to FEL evidence, did involve the FEL indirectly.

JEAN CHARLES DE MENEZES

To my mind, the one physical casualty of the 21/7 bombers was Jean Charles de Menezes. My limited involvement was to be asked a few questions, both by the police and by counsel for the family in connection with the inquest. The questions were around the briefing given to the police, prior to the shooting, basically the same from both parties, and boiled down to: "Was the briefing given to the police correct to say that the devices could be easily hidden around the body and easily triggered?" This was particularly thinking about the smaller devices found in the Luton car, and the answer was – yes. "Could the larger devices have been reconfigured as a suicide vest, and hidden that way?" The answer was – possible in principle but complicated and unlikely in the time available.

And then the really tricky one: "Could they have been briefed thus?" –"If you have clear sight of his open hands, they are empty, and he does not move them, then no shot need be made." Aaaargh. Well… in a comfortable debate somewhere, I *might* agree with that, but the atmosphere at the time was anything but, so would I have dared to brief that (or advised anyone else to)? I truly couldn't say. But looking at it purely personally, and bearing in mind they were given a positive identification, is it even humanly possible to be so self-possessed in such an extreme situation, where the slightest twitch by the target might be leading to death or injury to you and those around you, that you could comply with that?

So, anyway, my overall take on the whole episode was that the key mistake was that he was wrongly identified to the police as one of the bombers, which I have nothing to say about. Except that I do know what the atmosphere was like at the time, for all involved, which was one of barely controlled panic as to where and what the next attack might be. And in situations like that, mistakes very easily happen. And who caused that situation? (That's rhetorical!)

APPLICATION TO APPEAL

After SO15 had gone off and got themselves someone to test for hydrogen peroxide concentration using IRMS, they had asked me if the FEL wanted to have a copy of his report. After some thought, I said OK, it might be interesting for our research team to see, since they were also researching the technique, albeit for different uses. Maybe discussions between them might be mutually beneficial in a research sense. But I was very clear to the police, this was specifically for research information – *we were absolutely not doing any form of peer review!* We had ruled ourselves out of this endeavour right at the start so we were, by definition, not expert enough to peer review any IRMS work.

My mistake here, was assuming that this was also fully understood by our research team. So I was first taken aback, and then utterly pissed off, when I was presented, out of the blue, with a written report by our research team on the IRMS report – which picked out some significant flaws. I don't do apoplectic, but if I did, this would certainly have triggered it. This is still quite difficult for me write about because I liked and respected the people in our research team, but for me this smacked of normally professional people indulging in a bit of schoolboy playground one-upmanship. Admittedly, the IRMS guy was not the easiest person to work with, possibly because he didn't regard the FEL research team as peers – see my previous and following comments about academics and forensic scientists – but I thought our research team should have been a bit more grown up about this, and simply had a discussion with him, along the lines of – "We're not sure about that bit," and "Can you explain this bit here?" And then left him to do whatever he chose with his report.

Now this is just a personal (and no doubt controversial) view, but I think academics can be somewhat egocentric compared to forensic scientists – not because they are more subject to such character traits, but because forensic scientists are severely constrained by the environment they work in. All reputable forensic science labs have a hugely detailed quality system, which closely defines how every aspect of their work should be done; the methods, the processes, the management policies, the training and accreditation of the staff, everything. And this is born of bitter experience over many years of presenting evidence in court, and constantly trying not to repeat mistakes, many caused by the human foibles that we are all subject to. This was not the background that the IRMS expert came from. He was an academic, and academics do not generally work like this – indeed it could be argued that such constraints are counter-productive to good academic work, at least in its early stages.

Anyway, I now had a problem I really didn't need, just before the trial! The fact that the FEL had produced a written document, on a piece of work to be produced in court, even though it was not FEL work, meant that this had to be treated as a potentially disclosable document for the trial. And on a subject I had been determined we would have nothing to do with! So, through gritted teeth, I arranged for a meeting to be held at the FEL, between our research team, me, the IRMS guy, and SO15. It was SO15 who were responsible for collating all the evidence for the prosecution, and they had disclosure officers specifically responsible for ensuring that all disclosure requirements in the case were fully met. So we had what I remember was a, perhaps unsurprisingly, somewhat tense meeting. But all the points in our research team's document were raised, notes were made by all concerned – and that, as far as I was concerned, was my job done. SO15 could report back to their management and disclosure team, the IRMS guy could take away our observations and amend his report, or not, as he saw fit. And produce an amended report he did.

A pain, but all sorted then? Well, again, not quite. What I should also have made sure of, was that I gave the actual document to the police, and had them sign for it. But I didn't. I was too relieved just to have got the whole episode out of the way and get back to whatever I was doing at the time, that I overlooked that small step. They certainly had all the information that was in the document, but did they have the actual document? Probably – it was certainly present at the meeting – but I can't be certain.

Back to my question above – why does any of this matter? Well, it turns out that the defence did not have sight of this document prior to the trial. Then, in 2010, a member of the FEL research team resigned from the laboratory. Sometime later, he contacted one of the 21/7 trial defence team, and told him about the FEL IRMS document, which then formed the basis of an application to appeal. This caused us a lot of hassle in the lab, going back through meeting notes, emails, documents, letters, etc., then having a mini internal inquiry, ultimately concluding that no one had contravened any mandated processes, only in hindsight could things perhaps have been dealt with better, and we made all this available to anyone who should want it. And moved on.

But what did I actually feel about this? As per usual, I just did what I needed to, and then just packed it all away in some 'Room 101' in my brain, not to be looked at again. And this must have been some bloody big room by now, and was bulging at the seams. But looking back, if I'm honest, I was really quite angry. This was all from someone I counted a friend – still would like to. But this felt like a bit of a betrayal really. He didn't know anything more after he left, than he did before; he had watched the same trial we had, knew all about the report, knew what had (and hadn't) happened during the trial, everything. Yet it was only after he left, several years after the end of the trial, that he chose to raise it, and even then not with us in the lab. This was raised by him as a potential miscarriage of justice. Cobblers! It was, at worst, a technical discrepancy in procedure, at least as far as the FEL was concerned – I can't speak for other organisations. As far as a *real* miscarriage goes, this was nothing of the sort. The IRMS was *always* a giant red herring, which was always going to be arguable, whatever the result. But there was plenty of good reliable scientific evidence about the viability of the scene material, which was to my mind clear and unarguable. Yes, the document should have been disclosed to the defence. And it wasn't. I don't know why. Sometimes non-disclosure can have significant consequences on a trial outcome, so, as a principle, it shouldn't happen. But in this particular case, the actual consequences, in my opinion, are nil. But he knew all this years before he spoke up, so this all smacked of a bit of self-righteousness to me.

Anyway, I can't now remember the chronology of all this, I'm fairly sure I knew that the legal process was under way while I was still at the FEL, but I retired in 2013, and I don't think anything had actually happened in court by then. In any event, it was in 2015 that it finally came before the High Court, where three very senior judges ruled that the appeal would not be allowed on these grounds.

Is that the end of it? Probably not, a paper has recently done another article on it, so I daresay there will be some more legal stuff to come. But it's been long enough, and now that I've decided to write about my whole experience with 7/7 and 21/7,

I think it has done some good for my soul, and actually has been illuminating to me in ways I had not expected when I started it. So I no longer care about what anyone else might think I should or shouldn't say. This is not a technical treatise, this is some reflections on a personal journey through a very intense period of my life. And to continue with the concept of a 'Room 101' for a moment, I would say I have tugged on that door a couple of times in the narrative – and then firmly shut it again. I'm not sure what good would come from looking in there again now, but at least I am now aware it's there – which I wasn't before I started this. Yes, I learned a lot professionally throughout this period, but now I think I may have paid a higher personal cost than I knew then, or I could maybe have alleviated some of it if I had been more aware of it at the time. Never forgetting that, quite apart from the direct victims, there will be hundreds, maybe thousands, who will have been touched indirectly by those events in their own individual ways. Probably most of them to a far greater extent than me.